MARCO ⊕ POLO

Travel with **Insider Tips**

CR

Brown's Road

MK
ALBA.
○ Thessaloníki
Sea

TURKEY

Athens
GREECE
Iráklio
Crete
Cyprus

Mediterranean Sea

LIBYA
EGYPT

www.marco-polo.com

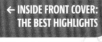

SYMBOLS

INSIDER TIP Insider Tip

★ Highlight

●●●● Best of ...

☼ Scenic view

☺ Responsible travel: for ecological or fair trade aspects

(*) Telephone numbers that are not toll-free

PRICE CATEGORIES HOTELS

Expensive over 100 euros

Moderate 60–100 euros

Budget under 60 euros

Prices for a double room. Hotels in the upper price range are often cheaper if you choose an all-inclusive package deal

PRICE CATEGORIES RESTAURANTS

Expensive over 16 euros

Moderate 12–16 euros

Budget under 12 euros

Prices include a main dish with side dishes and salad. Fish can be expensive

On the cover: Knossós and the labyrinth of the Minotaur p. 65, 22 | The longest canyon in Europe p. 107

CONTENTS

Ágios Nikólaos → p. 72

Ierápetra → p. 84

Sitía → p. 92

Road atlas → p. 132

MAPS IN THE GUIDEBOOK
(134 A1) Page numbers
and coordinates refer to
the road atlas
Map of the palace of
Knossós → p. 66
Maps of Chaniá, Réthimno,
Ágios Nikólaos, and Iráklio
inside the back cover

Coordinates are also given for
places that are not marked
on the road atlas

INSIDE BACK COVER:
PULL-OUT MAP →

PULL-OUT MAP 𝄁
(𝄁 A–B 2–3) Refers to the
removable pull-out map

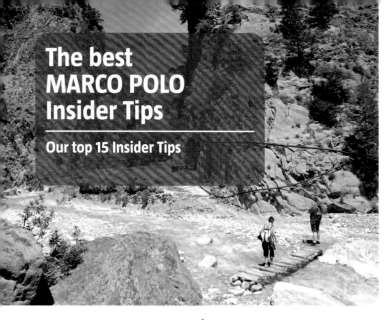

The best
MARCO POLO
Insider Tips

Our top 15 Insider Tips

INSIDER TIP **Culture at its finest**

Among the many summer culture festivals on the island, the Réthimno Renaissance Festival is the most ambitious. Within the impressive walls of the Venetian fortress the Renaissance Serenissima era comes alive with a varied programme of concerts, music and theatre pieces → p. 117

INSIDER TIP **A real farmer's market**

Every Saturday the lively farming village of Míres has a large farmer's market, well away from the tourist bustle → p. 71

INSIDER TIP **Family-friendly gorge**

Wandering through the Iríni Gorge is easy – even with young children – and it is usually open even when the famous Samariá Gorge is closed due to rockfall hazards. When you reach the end you can take a public bus or taxi back to the starting point → p. 42

INSIDER TIP **Where peace reigns**

Alison and her husband Stávros ensure that no noise disturbs their guests at their hotel Pórto Loutró → p. 43

INSIDER TIP **The sound of the lyre**

Local musicians like to perform in front of their home crowd in Terirém and Iráklio on their free weekends with their traditional *lýra* and *laouto* → p. 63

INSIDER TIP **Avocado beauty**

In the peaceful mountain village of Argiroúpoli Cretan avocados are processed into cosmetics and coffee and cocoa powder substitutes are produced from locally grown carob tree pods → p. 54

INSIDER TIP **A priest with a passion for collecting**

In Asómatos, Pápa Michális has an eclectic private collection and his daughter-in-law Sísi knows the history of every object → p. 55

INSIDER TIP **Silent, bright nights**

The heavens above the Lassíthi Plateau are full of stars and the silence quite overwhelming. In the restored Villaéti houses in Ágios Konstantínos you can experience both → p. 81

INSIDER TIP **Freshwater alternative**

The freshest salmon and rainbow trout is served at the trout farms of Zarós at Psilorítis → p. 71

INSIDER TIP **Enjoy Samariá**

To enjoy Crete's longest gorge without the masses it is best to overnight on the Omalós Plateau and be there before the tourist buses arrive (photo left) → p. 44

INSIDER TIP **Cretan Villa**

This villa was originally used as Ierápetra's hospital but today it is one of the most popular meeting places on the island. Manólis, the friendly landlord, treats his guests as though they are family → p. 87

INSIDER TIP **Fata Morgana**

In the stony landscape of Káto Zákros, Stella's Apartments seem like a mirage – blue and white houses in a lush garden → p. 99

INSIDER TIP **Guaranteed adrenaline rush**

In Arádena on the south coast the brave can do a 138 m (454 ft) bungee jump → p. 108

INSIDER TIP **Walk with Manólis**

Tour guide Manólis Kagiannákis offers tourists in Réthimno and surrounds day trips and excursions on foot or on mountain bike → p. 52

INSIDER TIP **Out of bed and into water**

Only a handful of hotels on Crete are right on the beach and Maria's Apartments in Frangokastéllo is one of the few. Here the Libyan Sea is like a flat and shallow paddling pool that makes it absolutely ideal for families with small children → p. 41

BEST OF ...

FOR FREE

● *The fishermen mosaic in Chersónisos*

Why pay museum entrance fees when art is available on the street? On the beach promenade at Chersónisos you can see a Roman mosaic of fishermen and their abundant catch → p. 64

● *Sightseeing through Chaniá*

Every half hour there are free sightseeing tours that leave from the market place – the best time is in the early evening when the street lights are slowly turned on → p. 36

● *Iráklio: poet's wall*

In other cities you may have to pay to enter the medieval city walls but not so in Iráklio. The only entrance is at the Martinengo Bastion where you will also find the tomb of the poet Níkos Kazantzákis with his epitaph: 'I hope for nothing, I fear nothing, I am free' → p. 61

● *Where the olive oil flows*

The young proprietor of the Paráskis olive oil factory will show you the secrets of harvesting olive oil and you can also go on a free guided tour of the ultra modern facility in Melidóni → p. 56

● *Minoan city*

The only Minoan city whose ruins you can visit free of charge is the one on Chióna beach at Palékastro. Investigate the ancient road network, the outlines of the houses and their drainage system → p. 99

● *Górtis: ruins in an olive grove*

After seeing the Odéon and Títus Basilica of Górtis, many travel further and miss out on the lovely walk through the ruins of the Roman city, which lies between age-old olive groves and – unlike the excavations on the opposite side of the road – they are also free of charge (photo) → p. 71

●●●● Dots in guidebook refer to 'Best of ...' tips

● *The sound of lyres in Chaniá*
The lýra and *laouto* are Crete's traditional musical instruments. Every night you can hear them being played in the taverna Kriti in Chaniá's old town. The lyrics are mostly about love and the fight for freedom → p. 37

● *Vámos: live in the town*
If you rent one of the restored houses in Vámos you will be in the centre of the town's day-to-day life, enjoy regional specialities in some of Crete's best tavernas and discover Crete's nature during walks → p. 45

● *Raki and mezédes*
When *mezédes* (photo) are served your table will be laden with a variety of small dishes. As an accompaniment to the tasty morsels Cretans love to drink *rakí* from small decanters. The ideal venue for this is called *rakádika* and a number of them are squeezed into the Odós Vernárdou in Réthimno. The *mezédes* in Ousíes are extremely well prepared → p. 51

● *Visit a potter's village*
In Margarítes – for centuries the pottery stronghold of the island – there are a number of small ceramics studios where you can still find traditional and modern pottery and souvenirs. Do not miss the last studio on the road to Eléftherna, where they still produce the large *píthoi* → p. 55

● *Surrounded by mountains*
Uninhabited plateaus are a geographic characteristic of the island. During the summer countless sheep and goats graze here and during the winter they are covered in snow. The Nída Plateau just under the summit of mount Psilorítis is easy to reach and beautiful to stroll through → p. 68

● *Nightlife in Iráklio*
In the street cafés surrounding the *Platía Korái* in the heart of Iráklio, young Cretans sit on trendy lounge furniture, meet their friends and listen to music. The popular drink from early morning until late at night is iced coffee → p. 63

ONLY IN

BEST OF ...

● *Marine life*
When it is raining visit Greece's most modern aquarium. There are over 2500 creatures in the *CretAquarium* in Goúrnes, among them octopus, lobsters, seahorses and sharks → p. 65

● *Just dive in*
Rainy days are ideal for scuba diving – children can learn using special equipment in the hotel pool and adults in the open sea – use an outfit like the *Atlantis Diving Centre* in Réthimno → p. 109

● *Market shopping in Chaniá*
In the *historic municipal market* in Chaniá – the most beautiful in Crete – you can stock up on Cretan specialities and then wait in one of the small quaint market tavernas for the showers to pass → p. 36

● *Glass blowers*
Visit one of Crete's largest glass workshops in Kókkino Chorió, where you can watch the *glass blowers* create colourful lamps, bowls, glasses and jewellery from recycled glass (photo) → p. 40

● *Descend into the underworld of Zoniá*
Descend 550 m into the underworld of stalagmites and stalactites in the *caves of Zoniá* – and discover the beautiful forms created by water → p. 68

● *Tóplou: monastery and mocha*
You will forget about time when you browse the valuable 14th century frescoes and icons in the *Tóplou Monastery* on the far eastern side of Crete. Then stop in at the charming adjoining *kafenío* for a dry rest and an espresso → p. 100

RAIN

RELAX AND CHILL OUT
Take it easy and spoil yourself

● *Feel the earth's forces at Ágios Pávlos*
Between Ágios Pávlos and Préveli on the south coast, you can feel the exceptional forces of the earth. Because of this workshops for yoga, meditation and t'ai chi are often held here → **p. 111**

● *Back to nature*
There are 13 restored natural stone houses in Miliá. Candles are used at night, drinking water is carried from a nearby fountain and the village taverna takes care of your well-being with produce and fresh ingredients from the region (photo). You will not hear a motor car, nothing disturbs the peace in this eco-village → **p. 44**

● *Seventh heaven in Eloúnda's spa*
Many luxury hotels also offer non-residents entrance to their spa facilities and one of the best is the *Blue Palace Resort Spa* in Eloúnda – unfortunately also pricey → **p. 79**

● *Comfortable train trip*
Have you ever had a ride in a *trenáki*? This mini train with three carriages trundles on rubber wheels across many Cretan country roads. You sit in open mini-carriages, feel the wind through your hair and arrive at your destination completely stress-free. The excursion programme is especially extensive in Georgioúpoli → **p. 114**

● *Relax with Hollywood stars*
Get yourself a drink at the bar and enjoy an evening in an outdoor cinema. The best is the summer *cinema Astéria* in Réthimno's old town where where Hollywood movies are shown beneath the Venetian fortress walls → **p. 52**

● *Venéto in Iráklio*
For a romantic aperitif or nightcap for two, you will find no better place in Iráklio than *Venéto's terrace*. Accompanied by discreet music, you can enjoy the soft evening breeze and the lights of the fishing boats in the harbour → **p. 63**

INTRODUCTION

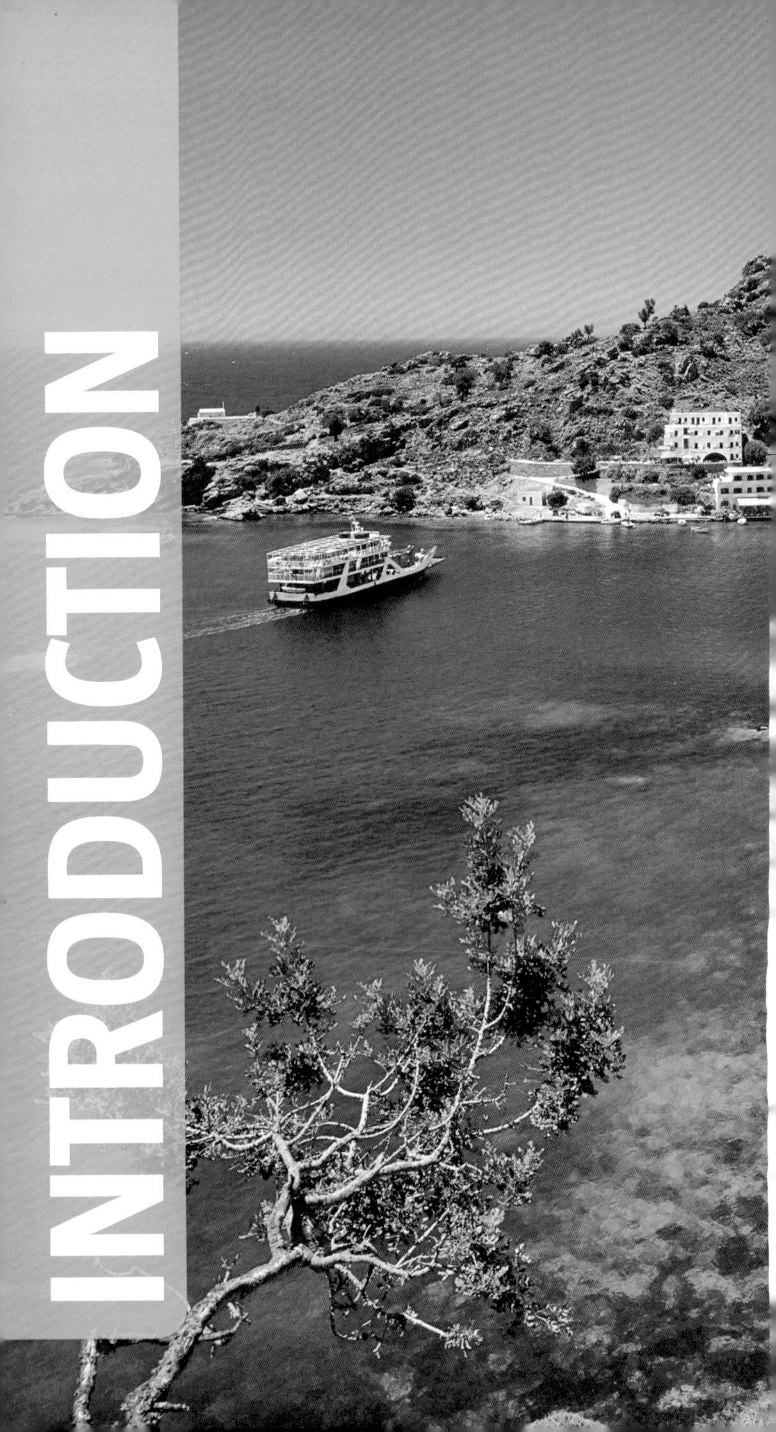

DISCOVER CRETE!

Crete is a world in itself. With its 2500 m (8200 ft) peaks, Greece's largest island rises out of the sea like a massive mountain. Here, everyone finds what they are looking for: long stretches of sandy beaches and isolated coves, a vibrant nightlife, the silence of wild gorges as well as various opportunities for biking, playing golf, surfing or diving. And the island offers a lot culturally because it is also home to one of Europe's oldest civilizations.

Towns and holiday resorts have moved with the times, but in the mountain villages, life is still very traditional. And so it goes in a small sleepy town in the Cretan mountains. It is still early in the year. In the modest *kafenío* at the platía, the coffee shop on the town square, wood is crackling in the fireplace. Chairs with woven seats line three of the walls. Against the fourth wall, behind the counter, the host brews rich

Photo: Coastal resort Loutró near Chaniá

Crete's interior with mountain villages and beautiful monasteries is as diverse as the coast

coffee in brass and copper pots and pours it into small espresso cups and serves it to the guests with a glass of water. Just above the counter is a huge flat screen television – made in Japan – broadcasting an important soccer match. Everyone is watching and commentating. Then the half-time whistle. A guest turns off the television. Two young men, both in Cretan OFI Iráklio shirts, grab their *lýras*, an age-old Cretan instrument, and begin playing and singing masterfully. Crete becomes

During half-time, two young men grab their *lýras*

1900–1450 BC
Minoan era. The Minoans built cities and huge palaces and across Crete, estates and farms were established

1450–650 BC
After the downfall of the Minoan culture, Greek tribes settled on the island. About 100 independent city states were founded

650–332 BC
Archaic and Classic era. The fortified cities of Crete feud amongst each other

332–67 BC
Hellenic era

67 BC–395 AD
Roman era

tangible through all the senses. After 15 minutes, the television is turned on again, the music dies down. An American fast-food chain advertises their hamburgers, and then the soccer players continue their game.

Yet even on Crete time does not stand still. Huge wind turbines can be seen on the mountain ridges and along the whole northern coast a wide motorway now shortens your trip. Quad bikes now roar through the narrow alleyways of Mália, a few miles from the Aegean coast there are now water parks with loud music and giant water-slides. For holidaymakers who prefer being taken care of there are a number of all-inclusive hotels and holiday resorts and one luxury hotel in Eloúnda even offers helicopter transfers and butler services with

> **Crete is part of the globalised world and aims to keep it that way**

the holiday villa that also comes with a private pool. In Iráklio an EU institute takes care of the data security of the whole of Europe, while on the south coast Chinese investors want to build a large container ship harbour for the distribution of their wares in the Mediterranean and Black Seas. On the Lassíthi Plateau, Albanian migrant workers harvest organically grown potatoes and the Pakistani shepherds can phone home to their hearts' content because of a flat rate. Crete is now very much a part of the globalised world and wants to keep it that way.

But Crete also has another interesting and distinctive side. Travelling from the airport, one cannot help but notice the bullet holes in the street signs. They have served as target practice for many Cretans. Every shot is an expression of the locals' unease over too much state authority. The small mountain village of Zoni400 made headlines when citizens protested against a large police presence after a narcotics investigation – according to them the sight of all the uniforms would have a negative impact on the children. This situation must have felt like an echo from their past under foreign rule: until Crete's union with Greece in 1912 and during the German occupation (1941–44) every act of resistance was seen as an act of bravery and is still praised in school text books. To this day the Cretan motto remains: 'Freedom or death!'

Despite this behaviour Crete remains one of the safest holiday destinations in the world. For centuries, hospitality has been one of their top priorities and as a tourist

395–1204 Byzantine era. Constantinople rules Crete	1204–1669 Venetian era	1669–1898 Turkish era. 1898 Independence: Prince George, second son of the Greek king, rules by order of the Sultan	1913 Union with liberated Greece	1941–1944 German invasion follows after an intense guerrilla war, in which German troops murdered many civilians

you will always experience it – certainly when you are away from the tourist centres. *Rakí* and fruit are served as dessert free of charge in most tavernas where the owner also often invites the guests to a cup of Greek coffee. And if you should stumble on a village wedding, you may well be invited to stay and join in with the celebrations.

Around 600,000 people live on the island with more than 150,000 of them in the northern part around the capital Iráklio, where the infrastructure struggles to handle that number of people. The other island cities are also situated mostly on the northern coast. Chaniá and Réthimno should definitely be on your sightseeing list: both places have picturesque harbours, Venetian royal palaces and narrow alleyways, mosques with tall minarets and inviting shopping streets. In the east is Ágios Nikólaos with its lovely location on the Gulf of Mirabéllo and a small lake directly next to the harbour, while the nearby Sitía has a serene landscape and a relaxed atmosphere. On the south coast, next to the Libyan Sea, there is only enough space for one city, which has an African flavour to it: Ierápetra.

The island's interior is just as diverse as the coast. Four mountain ranges define Crete: the White Mountains with its 2453 m (8043 ft) high Páchnes summit in the west, just east of the White Mountains, Mount Ída with the 2456 m (8056 ft) high Timíos Stávros summit, then in the eastern centre the 2148 m (7045 ft) high Díkti range and finally in the far eastern side the 1476 m (4841 ft) high Sitía Mountains. In between these mountain ranges, a whole range of hidden plateaus are completely cut off from the sea. Certain plateaus like Lassíthi and Chandrás are farmed intensively all year round, but on some like Nída or the Thriptí plateaus, farmers only move there during the summer.

Beaches, isolated mountain villages and Minoan history

It is possible to get to know Crete in a very short time. The island is quite big, 260 km (161½ mi) long and up to 60 km (37 mi) wide, but the different aspects are located close to each other. Day trips from the beaches and busy seaside resorts on the coast take you into isolated mountain villages and historic old towns, to the excavations of Minoan estates and temples. There are boat trips to off shore islands and guided mountain bike tours to experience nature. In the mountains of the surround-

1967–1974
Military dictatorship in Greece

1981
Greece joins the European Union

2002
The euro replaces the drachma as currency

2004
Athens hosts the Olympic Games

2010/2011
Greece can only be saved from bankruptcy through credit grants by European countries and the IMF. Loans, stipends and interest were lowered, while taxes increased

ing plateaus, you will see more sheep and goats than people. You can hike through mountains and gorges, but you can also play golf, practice yoga or meditate. And as for swimming, there are beaches for every taste: from west coast lagoons with turquoise blue water and sandy beaches to the palm tree lined beaches of Vái in the east. There are sand dunes and colourful pebble beaches between jagged steep stretches of coast, pretty coves and endless water sport possibilities. No entrance fees are charged on the island's beaches because freedom-loving Cretans are not interested in resort taxes and private beaches.

Crete is also unsurpassed as a destination for those wanting a study tour. Especially for its unique relics from the Minoan era that are 3500 to 4000 years old. The former palace cities of Knossós, Festós, Mália, Káto Zákros and Agía Triáda all bear evidence of the first civilization on European ground. Crete's archaeological museum shows that people from these prehistoric times possessed just as much art sense as we do today. Classic Grecian

Unique: the advanced civilisation of the Minoans

and Roman excavation sites in the countryside are also fascinating and there are almost 1000 churches and chapels that date back to the Byzantine era, some of them decorated with medieval frescoes.

The Venetians, who ruled Crete for almost 300 years after this, also had an important influence on the cities and the landscape. Venice promoted the cultivation of olive trees for oil to light up their palaces. They built impressive castles and surrounded cities with massive defensive walls some of which still exist. After the fall of Constantinople in 1453, Crete became the place of exile for Greek aristocrats and artists for the next 200 years. The exchange

> **The Venetians also shaped Crete's cities and landscape**

with Italy brought with it elements of the Renaissance visible in Cretan art. Many Turkish buildings, (the Turkish drove the Venetians from the island) give the cities of Chaniá, Réthimno and Ierápetra a strong oriental influence. As the home of so much cultural and history, the island has a lot more to offer than you would find in a normal holiday – another good reason to revisit Crete again and again.

WHAT'S HOT

1 Old meets new

Arts and crafts The designs may be extravagant, but the techniques are traditional. Cretan artists are rediscovering old techniques. Like *Manólis Patramánis*, who has devoted himself to mosaics and ceramics. Or *Mário Chalkiadáki* and *Natássa Papadogamvráki,* whose modern glass art is exhibited in museums *(Anogea, Réthimno, www.tarrhaglass. com, photo)*. At *Karoupis Art (Alexi Minoti 7, Koutouloufari, Chersónisos, www.kouroupis. gr)* a large selection of artwork by local artists is on offer.

Meat free

2

Vegetarian fare Vegetarians need not steer clear of Crete. The best vegetarian dishes are prepared in the *Vegera Taverna* where Vivi the proprietor prepares meatless versions of traditional Greek dishes like stuffed peppers – delicious! *(Zarós, www.zaros.info, photo)* The restaurant *To Trito Mati* is a big name in the alternative veggie-scene thanks to its fresh, simple and delicious food *(Paleochóra-Chaniá)*.

Mountain playground

3

Climbing The steep and rugged rock faces of the island are an El Dorado for rock climbers. *Cretan Adventures* organises climbing trips and also provides the equipment *(Odós Evans 10, Iráklio, www.cretanadventures.gr, photo)*. Those needing help to choose the right route or to find a guide, can contact the Association of Mountain Climbers of Rethymnon *(Dimokratias 12, Réthimno, www.eos.rethymnon.com)*. The hard core climbers can start at the guest house *Kofinas* in the small mountain farming village of Kapetaniana. Climbers will be rewarded with a spectacular view *(Kapetaniana 28, Asimi)*.

Your private pool

4

Exclusivity! Once you have experienced the luxury of a private pool, it is difficult not to expect it everywhere. In Crete the private pools trend is on the upswing. In the *St Nicolas Bay Resort Hotel & Villas* guests enjoy privacy in suites with large seawater swimming pools and generous gardens. As a welcoming gesture Champagne and Cretan delicacies are provided on arrival. *(Ágios Nikólaos, www.st nicolasbay.gr, photo).* The villas in the *Mythos Palace Resort Spa* not only have their own private swimming pool, but also a breathtaking view of the open sea. Why should you even leave your villa? *(Kavros Apokoronou, Georgioúpolis, www.mythos-palace.gr)* Also, in the *Iti Aquis Blue Sea Resort & Spa* people staying in the suites do not have to worry about reserving deckchairs as even the smaller suites come with their own private pool.

Grey and docile

5

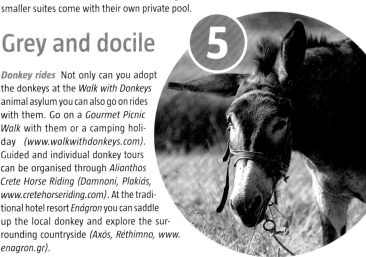

Donkey rides Not only can you adopt the donkeys at the *Walk with Donkeys* animal asylum you can also go on rides with them. Go on a *Gourmet Picnic Walk* with them or a camping holiday *(www.walkwithdonkeys.com).* Guided and individual donkey tours can be organised through *Alianthos Crete Horse Riding (Damnoni, Plakiás, www.cretehorseriding.com).* At the traditional hotel resort *Enágron* you can saddle up the local donkey and explore the surrounding countryside *(Axós, Réthimno, www. enagron.gr).*

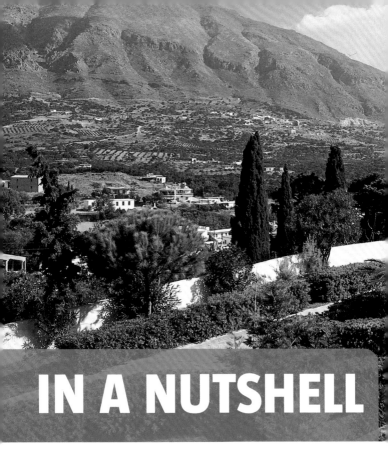

IN A NUTSHELL

ALTERNATIVE ENERGY

Not only is Crete blessed with lots of sun, but it also has lots of wind. This has been put to good use to harvest energy through various wind generators (made of sailing material) on the Lassíthi Plateau. The large wind generators are used to generate energy for the island, while solar energy is used by private houses and hotels for water heating. Private power suppliers use wind energy to supplement the power supplied by the Public Power Company (DEI) which still uses mazut, an extremely cheap but environmentally harmful oil derivative.

BYZANTINE

You will see the Byzantine influence everywhere you go in Crete. There are Byzantine churches, castle ruins and in churches you will see the Byzantine double eagle, a symbol of the church (which has survived) and the empire that floundered. Byzantium was invaded by the Turks in 1453 and renamed Istanbul. The Greeks established the city as Byzantine in 660 BC and Emperor Constantine moved the capital of the Roman Empire there in 330 BC. When Emperor Theodosius divided the empire in 395 BC, the city became Constantinople and was the centre of the Byzantine Empire.

Photo: Chapel in Lefkógia a village in southern Crete

Romans and Venetians, Turks, tourists and tomato growers – despite many invaders the island has preserved its own unique character

While Rome and the Western Roman empire fell during the 5th century, the Byzantine Emperor kept and expanded his empire. Under Emperor Justinian I (527–565) the empire reached as far as Italy, North Africa and Asia Minor.

Orthodox Christianity was the state religion and Greek the state language of the Byzantine empire. When Venetian and European crusaders plundered the city of Byzantium, and stripped the Byzantine empire of its power, Crete fell under foreign domination for more than 700 years. They kept their identity intact, because they continued to regard themselves as Byzantines.

DANCE

Traditional Cretan dance is still practiced today, even by younger Cretans. Not only is it still seen at folk festivals, but also at christenings and weddings, village celebrations and even in nightclubs. The *pentozális* is danced only by men but women also participate in the *chaniótiko*. Both are circle dances with some solo parts. A typical dance for couples is the *soústa*.

ENVIRONMENTAL PROTECTION

Environmental protection in Crete is slowly but surely gaining ground due to financial support from the European Union and committed young people. Cities are building environmentally sound sewage plants; hotel chains like Grecotel have realised that being eco-friendly has advertising appeal. Nevertheless, environmental awareness amongst the Cretan population is still very poor, as shown by the numerous illegal dump sites and rampant use of plastic.

FAUNA

The only large wild mammal is the Cretan wild goat (locally called the *kri-kri*, from the scientific name *Capra aegagrus cretica*). They still roam in inaccessible parts of the White Mountains and in some parts of the small islands Día, Ágii Pántes and Ágii Theodóri. The best place to see the *kri-kri* is in the city parks of Chaniá and Réthimno. The sandy beaches of Crete are home to turtles *Caretta caretta* who lay their eggs during midsummer but their habitat is now seriously threatened by tourism. Clearly heard – but hard to

In spring Crete's landscape comes into its own: the lush green Lassíthi Plateau

see – are the cicadas singing undisturbed in the trees through summer.

FLORA

Between April and June, Crete soil displays just what it can produce when there is enough water. Fruit trees, almond trees, pomegranate and gorse, oleander and chestnut trees all flourish here. The pastures and meadows are covered in poppies, asphodel, anemones, narcissus, cyclamen and wild tulips, the mountains covered in fragrant herbs like thyme and oregano and scattered between them are bright white, pink and purple rock roses. During the summer, the vines are heavy with grapes, which along with the 15 million olive trees are the most important agricultural plant on the island. Also in the coastal regions are citrus fruits, bananas and avocados. Flax, cereals and vegetables are also grown.

In the higher regions, pines, oaks and maple trees thrive and closer to the coast are cypresses, sycamores and eucalyptus trees and often planted along lanes. In gardens medlar trees and every kind of fruit are grown while on the beaches you will find tamarisks and sometimes Cretan palms (similar to date palms) like those growing in Vái or Préveli.

GREENHOUSES

Naturally it was a Dutchman who taught the Cretans to grow tomatoes and early vegetables in greenhouses in the 1960s. Thanks to the Cretan sun the produce does not need to be heated, just watered. These greenhouses are not covered with glass but with plastic sheeting. When they can no longer be used, they are just left there for the wind to shred the plastic and blow it away: refuse disposal the Greek way. Whole tracts of land have been turned into plastic deserts that glisten like water in the sun.

Icon painters follow strict traditions

ICONS

In the Greek Orthodox Church, images of saints and biblical events on panels are called icons. They can be found in Crete's churches but also in private homes, on the dashboards of buses, in the wheelhouses of fishing boats and on the bridges of large ferries.

Icons are the 'doors to heaven' because the saints enter into homes through them and they therefore enjoy great reverence. They are decorated with precious metals, expensive fabrics, precious stones, rings and watches. Just like the fresco painters, icon painters must abide by ancient and strict rules. They have very little creative freedom and imagination and creativity are not required.

LÝRA & LAOÚTO

Cretan music can be heard on all Cretan radio stations, in tavernas and festivals and it has fans across all age groups. The typical instruments from Cretan folklore are the three-stringed pear-shaped *lýra* (lyre) and the *laoúto* (lute), a five stringed, long-necked plucking instrument. Pure instrumental pieces are rarely played. *Lýra* players mostly celebrate with a form of monotonous chanting and rhyming couplets called *mantinádes* and *rizítika*. There are many classics, but often these verses are improvised for special occasions and those present.

MINOS & MINOTAUR

What the Cretans called their rulers during the second century BC, we will never know. We do know that during the first century BC in the Greek mythology, he was called Minos and that Minos was also the name of the founder of the Minoan empire. The Greeks saw him as the son of Zeus and the Phoenician princess Europa, who Zeus – in the guise of a bull – kidnapped and brought to Crete.

At the Minoan palace in Knossós is a labyrinth built by Daedelus – also known as the first human to be able to fly – which was built to hold the Minotaur, a monster with the head of a bull and the body of a human. Every year seven young maids and men were sacrificed to it. The beast was the offspring of Minos' wife, Pasiphae and a bull that her husband had refused to sacrifice to the gods. The Athenian prince Thesues finally slayed the Minotaur and then made his way back out of the labyrinth with the help of Ariadne's string.

PALM DEATHS

During the second part of the last century, many hoteliers who wanted to shade their pool areas and hotel gardens, imported mature palm trees from Northern Africa and with them the red palm weevil, a beetle similar to a ladybird. They can smell palm trees from miles away, dig holes in the stems and then lay their eggs. The palm's branches turn yellow and have to be cut off. Precautions are now being taken all over Crete to combat the weevils but only time will tell whether or not these precautions are successful.

POLITICS

Traditionally Cretans vote left i. e. Socialist and Communist parties. Of the 300 seats in the predominantly social democratic Athenian Parliament, Crete has 16 seats. Ten represent the Social Democratic party the PASOK, five represent the conservative party Néa Dimokratía and one represents the Communist party KKE.

Thus far, Greece has been a strictly centralist governed country, in which the smaller regions hardly had a say and very few of their own financial resources. This is set to change over the course of the Kallikrátis administrative reforms which should be completed by 2013.

RAKÍ

Rakí is the national drink of Crete. This clear grape schnapps, made from pressed grapes, can be found in all *kafenías* and in many hotels. Taste it and you will understand why Cretan men attribute their strength and fighting spirit to this strong drink.

RELIGION

The majority of Cretans are Greek Orthodox Christians. Everywhere on the island you will come across Orthodox priests, with their long dark robes, thick beards and headgear. The Orthodox priests are allowed to get married and

Every town has a church – testimony to the strong Greek Orthodox faith

often have large families. They are paid by the state.

Orthodox Christians do not recognise the Pope as the head of Christianity. They feel that they are closely connected to the apostles and the early Christians because they have not changed their beliefs since the 8th century. The official schism in the church came about in 1054.

UNIVERSITIES

The University of Crete which was founded in 1973 has campuses in Iráklio and Réthimno. The university has 25,000 students and 700 teachers. Greek high school graduates do not have a choice about the university they want to attend. Students are assigned to universities according to the marks they receive. Only the best attend university in Athens or Thessaloníki, the rest are sent to the provincial universities. So students from all over Greece study in Crete.

VENIZÉLOS

Elefthérios Venizélos, born 1864 in Chaniá, was one of Crete's most influential politicians. In 1898, he played a major role in the withdrawal of the Turks from the island and the struggle for Crete's union with Greece. In 1909 he was elected as Prime Minister and in this post contributed significantly to the establishment of a modern Greece. In most of the Cretan towns and villages, streets and squares are named after him. Elefthérios Venizélos died in 1936, and his grave, close to Chaniá is a national memorial.

FOOD & DRINK

Cretans almost never go out to eat alone or just with their partners. Food is a social matter – it tastes best with good company around a large table. And it is only natural that children are also part of it.

This dining community which the Cretans call *paréa* means that no one orders just for themselves. Instead a variety of salads and delicious starters are ordered and everyone then helps themselves. Then large platters of fish or grilled meat are ordered which are also put on the table for everyone to share. Most Cretans do without dessert, because the portions are so generous there are usually a lot of leftovers. It is not the done thing to clear the platters and plates completely as this is taken as being miserly.

As a tourist dining out alone or with a partner, you can of course order in the normal fashion – although the Cretan way is much more fun and you get to sample a variety of dishes. If the waiter does not clear away your plates as you dine it is because this is a sign to show the other diners that you can afford a lavish meal. By the way: it is the Cretan custom that one person usually pays for everyone, if this does not suit you then let the waiter know when you place your order.

Food the Cretan way: good dining in Crete means easy going conviviality around a large table

In the holiday resort areas Cretans have adapted to the customs of the holiday-makers by decorating the tavernas in the traditional way and bringing the food to the table hot. In recent years a number of restaurants have opened that serve haute cuisine. Their main clientele are the Cretans themselves but also Greek holidaymakers who value good regional cuisine.

So, everyone finds what they are looking for: from the simple, inexpensive little snack bars for *gyros* and *souvláki* to the upmarket Italian restaurants with Mediterranean cuisine, from the simple family tavernas with home cooking to Cretan gourmet restaurants with exquisite creations. No matter where you eat, if you order fresh fish, be prepared to pay high prices: you will not find anything

LOCAL SPECIALITIES

▶ **afélia** – pork casserole dish
▶ **briám** – oven baked aubergines and olive oil
▶ **choriátiki** – Greek tomato salad served with goat's cheese and olives
▶ **chtapódi** – squid, grilled, braised or as a cold salad
▶ **dákos** – the Cretan variation of bruschetta: finely chopped tomatoes, herbs, onions and oil served on toasted bread
▶ **dolmádes** – vine leaves filled with rice and minced meat, served hot with a béchamel sauce (photo left)
▶ **fakí** – lentil soup
▶ **fasoláda** – bean soup
▶ **fáva** – pureed yellow peas which the guest prepare themselves at the table with onions and olive oil (photo right)
▶ **gópes** – grilled sardines
▶ **jemistés** – tomatoes and peppers filled with rice and minced meat
▶ **juvétsi** – noodles with beef or lamb baked in an earthenware pot
▶ **kakaviá** – fish soup – guests choose their own fish
▶ **kalitsúnia** – pastry filled with spinach or chard and cream cheese
▶ **ksifía** – grilled swordfish

▶ **kúklus** – snails accompanied by a glass of *rakí*
▶ **lachanodolmádes** – small cabbage rolls filled with rice, minced meat and herbs and served with a béchamel sauce
▶ **marídes** – crispy fried anchovies
▶ **moussaká** – baked dish of minced meat, aubergines, potatoes and béchamel sauce
▶ **paidákia** – grilled lamb chops – best over wood coals
▶ **pantsária** – red beetroot, either served cold as a salad or hot with its leaves as a vegetable
▶ **pastítsjo** – baked dish made of macaroni, minced meat and béchamel sauce
▶ **patsá** – tripe soup
▶ **revithókeftédes** – potato pancakes or croquettes made from chickpea flour
▶ **Sfakiániés píttes** – a type of crêpe, filled with honey and cream cheese
▶ **sínglino** – lightly smoked pork
▶ **stifádo** – mostly beef (sometimes rabbit) stew in a tomato and cinnamon sauce with vegetables
▶ **supjés** – a type of squid

under 40 euros per kilo. When dining out, Cretans drink water and beer or wine. A wide variety of Cretan wines are available and the quality has improved substantially in recent years. Aside from wine by the glass and the affordable *rétsina* – Greek white wine infused with resin from the Aleppo pine – there are also a large number of quality wines from independent cellars. Wines from the co-operative wine cellars of Sitía and Péza near Iráklio are recommended. There are also some more exclusive wines in limited quantities available from independent cellars like *Lýrarákis*, *Económou*, *Manoussákis*, *Michalákis* and *Crétas Olympías cellars. Boutáris* is a quality wine produced throughout Greece.

Most tavernas and restaurants are open from 9am until well after midnight. Cretans seldom eat lunch before 1pm and at night you will find them with their *paréa* dining at 10pm or even later.

Lovers of sweet delicacies can visit a *zacharoplastío,* the Greek version of a confectionery. Here you will find a wide variety of tarts, pastries, pralines and oriental pastries like *baklavá* and *kataïfí,* which look sweeter than they actually are, and the favourite *milópita* (apple pie) which is often served with vanilla ice cream.

Cretan coffee houses are where the men meet. Every village has at least one *kafenío,* most have more *kafenía.* This is necessary because each *kafenío* is associated with one of the three main Greek political parties: the Conservatives, the Socialists or the Communists. Although operated by a private owner, the *kafenío* is something of a public institution. There is usually no obligation to order anything. The men sit down together to talk about God and the world and above all about Greek politics or to play *távli,* draughts or cards.

When you order a coffee for yourself, remember to say exactly how you prefer it. The Cretans drink Greek coffee which is coffee brewed together with water and sugar. *Kafé ellinikó* is served in many variations: *skétto,* without sugar; *métrio,* with some sugar; *glikó,* with lots of sugar; *dipló,* a double portion. Instant coffee is also always available. Basically you order it as *neskafé* and specify the amount of sugar you prefer. There is also the option of *neskafé sestó,* hot or *frappé,* cold Nescafé beaten to foam.

A classic: strong espresso, sweetened by a *baklavá*

Young Cretans love cold variants of coffee like *freddo espresso* and *freddo cappuccino,* and just like the Greek espresso, they are served with a glass of cold water.

SHOPPING

In the souvenir shops in the cities and resorts you will find lots of mass-produced goods that are seldom made in Crete. It is better to shop in the alleyways of Chaniá and Réthimno, the shops in Ágios Nikólaos, the crafters' workshops on roadsides and in the villages. Shop hours: in resort areas and during the peak season usually daily 10am–midnight, and in the cities Mon–Sat 10am–1.30pm, Tue, Thu and Fri also 5.30–8pm.

ARTS & CRAFTS

Coloured glass is a craft on the rise and there are glass artists everywhere in Greece. The large glassworks in Kókkino Chorió, 26 km (16 mi) east of Chaniá, is famous for its articles made from recycled glass. You will also find modern and traditional ceramics all over Crete. Margarítes, 27 km (16¼ mi) south-east of Réthimno is a potters' village well worth visiting. Carvings from olive wood are particularly valuable because the wood has to be cured for a long time and is very difficult to work with. The largest selection can be found in Mátala on the southern coast.

CULINARY DELIGHTS

Olives, olive oil and honey are healthy souvenirs which can also be bought in trendy health food shops. Fruit preserves, dried fruit and the many types of cheese are also typical of the island.

FABRICS & TEXTILES

Museums are where you will find precious embroidered and woven items as those sold in villages like Fódele are more often than not mass-produced.

FASHION

Cretan fashionistas fly to Athens for their shopping; only Iráklio offers a few international labels in the town centre. Cretan cities do however offer a wide variety of Greek shoe fashion.

ICONS

Old icons may only be exported with special permission. This is not necessary for newly painted icons. It is better to buy

Whether you are looking for arts and crafts or food, the selection of local souvenirs is extensive – you just have to know where to shop

directly from the icon painters who work in the old town of Iráklio.

JEWELLERY

In Crete you will still find some small gold and silversmiths – who still produce some of their wares themselves – in Chaniá's old town and the harbour at Ágios Nikólaos. Before you buy, always check the quality. It is best to decline the glass of oúzo offered by the salespersons so you can make a sober choice based on the stamp on the jewellery.

MUSEUM REPLICAS

Seldom do you find as many museum objects as in Crete but only a few will be authorised museum copies. The museum shop in the former Venetian loggia in Réthimno offers the widest variety and

they also ship larger objects anywhere in the world. A few jewellers opposite the archaeological museum in Iráklio also sell good (but unauthorised) copies of Minoan jewellery.

MUSIC

Whether it is traditional Cretan *lýra* sounds or the rock music of the Greek charts – you will find them in any music shop in Crete. Foreign CDs are very expensive in Crete.

SPIRITS & WINE

A good selection of Cretan wines are available in the cities from the speciality shops called *cáva*. Wine shops in Péza and Boutáris close to Iráklio also offer wine tastings. *Rakí* can be bought everywhere but because the quality differs it is better to sample it before you buy.

THE PERFECT ROUTE

CITY, COUNTRY, MONASTERY

The motorway, which starts at the airport, feeds straight into the heavy traffic of the island's capital Iráklio. For an hour or so you can enjoy views of the Aegean coast and the almost 2500 m (8200 ft) high Psilorítis Mountains. Only then will you drive inland to the ➊ *Arkádi Monastery* → p. 55, Crete's national shrine. With ➋ *Réthimno* → p. 47 and its Venetian harbour, the first Cretan city awaits you, with ➌ *Vámos* → p. 45 an authentic village full of local life. In the taverna *I Stérna tou Bloumósifis* on the main road, you can have a great Cretan meal.

WESTWARDS TO THE SOUTH SEA

➍ *Chaniá* → p. 33 scores points with its old town, interesting museums, small hotels in historical houses and numerous tavernas in winding alleys (photo left). ➎ *Kissámos* → p. 42 is a tranquil rural town, where boats depart for day trips to the Venetian fortress island ➏ *Gramvoúsa* → p. 43 where a South Sea-style lagoon awaits.

ON THE WAY TO CRETE'S LONGEST GORGE

The beautiful beach of ➐ *Elafonísi* → p. 40 offers fantastic blue and turquoise hues and fine sand. In ➑ *Paleochóra* → p. 44, the whole town centre turns into an open air taverna in the evening. Start your trip along the southern coast which also takes you into the mountains now and then. Then you can go for a hike in ➒ *Samariá* → p. 107 Crete's longest and most famous gorge.

IN THE WILD SFAKÍA

➓ *Chóra Sfakíon* → p. 40, the village and the harbour of the wild Sfakiá invite tourists with boat trips to beaches that can only be reached by foot or boat. In ⑪ *Frangokastéllo* → p. 41 the castle looks like a toy castle, it is right next to the most child friendly beach on the island. Adventurers can wade and swim from the beach ⑫ *Préveli* → p. 56 up the gorge of a cold mountain creek.

Experience the multiple facets of Crete, once around the island with detours into its mountainous interior

HIPPIE CAVES & MINOAN PALACE SETTLEMENT

⑬ Mátala → p. 69 was famous during the hippie-era – caves and an old fishing village line the beach. **⑭ Festós → p. 70** was once an important Minoan settlement on a hill in one of the island's most fertile plateaus, **⑮ Górtis → p. 70** capital of the island during Roman times.

IN THE EAST, A HINT OF AFRICA

The next destination is a small town in the east, **⑯ Ierápetra → p. 85** which has a North African feel to it. Isolated back roads take you to **⑰ Káto Zákros → p. 98** with its Minoan palace city, where tortoises lie in the sun and where you will find a long empty pebble beach. There is always something to do at **⑱ Vái → p. 100** Crete's largest palm grove beach (photo left).

VISIT ZEUS ON THE PLATEAU

⑲ Sitía → p. 92 is a peaceful town with a taverna-lined beach promenade. From here you can travel along the northern coast towards Iráklio via the beautiful provincial capital **⑳ Ágios Nikólaos → p. 73** with its picturesque lake. The last highlight on this trip is the **㉑ Lassíthi Plateau → p. 80** which is completely surrounded by mountains. Take a walk and discover the cave where Zeus was born and also some of the 20 or so villages.

Approx. 1100 km (683 mi). Driving time: 25 hours. Travel time: at least two weeks. Detailed map of the route on the back cover, in the road atlas and the pull-out map

CHANIÁ

The west of Crete is especially rich in contrasts. The beautiful Chaniá with its Venetian influenced old town has a very cultured, urbane atmosphere, in the White Mountains the island shows its harsher side, inviting you to walk through the gorges and small villages.

On its western coast are two lagoons like those found in the Caribbean and on the harbourless southern coast the few beaches are surrounded by inaccessible rocks. Valleys are filled with orange trees, old chestnut tree forests and olive groves with trees that are over 1000 years old and then there are the high peaks of the surrounding plateau, where countless sheep and goats graze, as well as the canyons with circling vultures. Archaeological excavations and old monasteries are found in the lonely landscape while life pulsates in Chaniá.

> **CITY** **WHERE TO START?**
> Parking close to the **old town** is scarce. The best option is at the north-western harbour exit at the platía Taló. Municipal buses stop at the market. The terminal for long distance buses is close to Platía 1866, from where the old town and harbour is just a five minute walk away.

Photo: Lefká Óri or the White Mountains

White Mountains, steep coasts: hike through the Iríni Gorge or take a boat out to the islands and coves in the diverse west

CHANIÁ

MAP INSIDE BACK COVER
(135 E3) (*M D2*) During the winter, the view of this vibrant city (population 53,400) is at its prettiest. The 2000 m (6560 ft) White Mountains peaks are sharp and clear and form a picturesque backdrop to the historic old town.

In the often hazy summer air, the mountains do not seem as high or as close. The ocean and long beaches which start in the city and reach far to the west, are far more prominent then.

During the summer, the historic Venetian and Turkish houses, tavernas and shops in the narrow winding alleys are at their busiest. In the old town you will also find many small hotels, often decorated in the

Painted sarcophagi in the
Archaeological Museum

Venetian or Cretan style. From many a
hotel balcony, you will have a view of the
long stretch of cafés and tavernas along
the port of ⭐ Chaniá's harbour where
today only leisure and excursion boats are
anchored. Parts of the historical city wall
remains, behind which the new city
stretches out. The new city is also home
to Crete's most beautiful city park – an
oasis in the centre of the busy traffic.

ÁGIOS NIKÓLAOS CHURCH

This Greek Orthodox Church could be the
only one in the world which is flanked on
the one side by a Christian clock tower
and on the other side by an Islamic minaret. The Ottomans converted the former
Dominican church into a mosque and after
the Greeks re-converted it again, they left
the minarets. During the last century it has
been restored which shows the improved
relationship between Greece and its former enemy, Turkey.

ARCHAEOLOGICAL MUSEUM

The museum is housed in a converted
Franciscan church in the Gothic style from
the Venetian era. Items from all the different historical eras found in and around
Chaniá are on display. Especially interesting are the late-Minoan painted sarcophagi and the coloured glass vessels found
in a woman's grave (4th century BC). The
imprint of the unique seal from the 15th
century BC is seen on the title page of the
museum's free catalogue. It shows the
glory of the former Minoan settlement
where the harbour is situated today. *April–
Oct Mon 1–7.30pm, Tue–Sun 8am–7.30pm,
Nov–March Tue–Sun 8.30am–3pm | en-
trance 2 euros | combi-ticket with Byzantine
Collection 3 euros | Odós Chalidón 25*

ARSENAL

At the harbour there are still nine of the
23 Venetian warehouses dating from the
15th century used by Venetian shipbuilders.
Today, they are mainly used as crafters'
workshops and sometimes exhibitions take
place here. *Admission free | Aktí Enosséos*

JANISSARY MOSQUE

This building dating back to 1645 was
named after the elite troops of the
Ottoman Sultan. Its minaret was demol-

ished in 1930 and the interior has mainly been used for various purposes from a souvenirs shop to an art gallery. *No interior viewing | Aktí Tombási*

MINOAN SHIP

On display in a former Venetian shipbuilding hall at the eastern end of the harbour is a replica of a 3500-year old Minoan ship. Its seaworthiness was tested in 2004 during a trip from Chaniá to Piraeus. It was built with exactly the same materials and tools that the Minoans used. *Daily 10am–4pm and 6–9 pm | entrance 2 euros | Odós Defkalónia*

NAUTICAL MUSEUM

A museum in the Fírkas fortress that houses displays of items from sea battles, navigation equipment, models of ships, portraits of important admirals and a lovely shell collection. *Daily 9am–4pm, in winter 10am–2pm | entrance 3 euros | Aktí Kundurióti*

CITY PARK

In Crete's most beautiful city park, you will be able to see Crete's wild goats up close. The park café *O Kípos (daily from 9am | Moderate)* is a traditional but elegant coffee house, where Greek espresso is still served in copper pots, but you can also order fine Champagne. *Odós Dimokratías/ Odós Tzanakáki*

ETZ HAYYIM SYNAGOGUE

A former Catholic Church converted into a synagogue in 1669. Today it serves as a memorial and museum for members of many religions. Thankfully it is situated across from a police station: in the winter of 2009/10, Greek, American and British neo-Nazis tried to set fire to the synagogue. *Mon, Tue, Thu, Fri 10am–5pm, Wed 10am–2pm | admission free, donations of 2 euros requested | Paródos Kondiláki | www.etz-hayyim-hania.org*

HISTORICAL & FOLK MUSEUM

A private folk museum filled with many historical objects and tools as well as life size wax figures in various scenes from everyday life over the centuries. *Rakí* distilleries and wine presses along with weaving looms, tailors' and cobblers' tools. The proprietor Aspasía Bikáki produces traditional lace which is sought after throughout Greece. *Mon–Sat 9am–3pm and 6–9pm | entrance 3 euros | Odós Chalidón 46 B*

FOOD & DRINK

KALI KARDIA – GOOD HEART

Cosy taverna in a former Jewish quarter with wine from the tap and pastries for dessert. *Daily 11am–2am | Odós Kondiláki 31 | Budget*

MONASTIRI

Taverna right on the harbour, serving seasonal and special Cretan dishes like cured pork *sínglino* and onion dishes like *volvoús*. *Daily from noon | Aktí Tombázi 12 | www.monastiri-taverna.gr | Moderate*

TAMAM

Taverna in what was once a Turkish bath, meeting place of the local intellectuals and artists. The food is a combination of recipes from the two important Greek cities that are now in Turkey, Smýrna (now Izmir) and Constantinople (now Istanbul). *Daily from 1pm | Odós Zambéliu 49 | www.tamamrestaurant.com | Moderate*

INSIDER TIP THE WELL OF THE TURK

An atmospheric restaurant hidden in a Turkish well. Inside the small interior, rare specialities from different regions of the former Ottoman Empire, Syria and Egypt are served. During the winter, live music is performed on Sundays. *Wed–Sun from 7pm | Odós Kalinikú Sarpáki 1–3, entrance from Odós Daskalojánnis | www.welloftheturk.com | Expensive*

SHOPPING

CARMELA
Tasteful shop with artistic ceramics, jewellery and paintings. *Odós Angélu 7*

ARTS AND CRAFTS
The heart of the arts and crafts area is in Topanás, the historic old town between the *Angélu, Zambéliu* and *Theotokopúlu* alleys.

MUNICIPAL MARKET ●
This century old building now also has souvenir sellers mixed in with the greengrocers and fishmongers. The most traditional and original aspect of the market are its quaint tavernas. *Mon–Sat 8.30am–1.30pm, Tue, Thu, Fri also 6–9pm | Platía Venizélos*

MAT
Athanásios Díamantópoulos sells a wide variety of chess and *távli* sets in his tiny shop. *Mon–Sat 9am–2pm, Mon–Fri also 4.30–8.30pm | Odós Potié 51*

ODÓS SKRÍDLOFF
This street which runs parallel with the city wall is crammed full of leather shops. Besides selling leather clothing, handbags and other accessories from Greek manufacturers, they also sell many fashionable Italian designs.

SPORTS & BEACHES

Swimming close to the city is not recommended due to Chaniá's sewage conditions.

LOW BUDGET

▶ The South Seas-style lagoons of *Bálos* – which can only be reached from Kíssamos by boat or a four-wheel drive plus a short walk – tolerates illegal camping. During the summer a taverna is open and this is the only place where you can get water. No better place to experience Crete's starry night sky!

▶ A free ● city roundtrip on a Chaniá council minibus takes you through parts of the old town, through the modern city centre, past the city park and back to the municipal market. Buses leave every half hour from the market from 9 am until 11pm.

Wide variety in Chaniá's municipal market – from fresh fish to souvenirs

Kalamáki, about 5 km (3½ mi) east of Chaniá is perfect for surfing. Mountain bikes can be hired from *Trekking Plan* in the suburb of Agía Marína.

The water park *Limnoupolis* is situated in the hills of Varípetro, 7 km (4¼ mi) from Chaniá. *May–Oct daily 10am–6pm | entrance 19 euros, children (6–12 years) 13 euros, after 3pm 10 euros | www.limnoupolis.gr | buses from Platía 1866*

ENTERTAINMENT

The place to visit in the evening is the old town area behind the harbour promenade and the area behind the Hotel Porto Veneziano. The music tavernas in the historic ruins are very authentic.

ÉLA ★
This Venetian house (which was destroyed by a fire in 1988 and is roofless) is now used by Adónis and Pános as a music taverna, and every evening there are *bouzoúki* and guitar performances. During the day extendable awnings provide shade. The menu offers a lot of Cretan specialities like the cream cheese *misíthra. Rakí* and fruit as dessert is on the house. *Daily 11am–1pm | Odós Kondiláki 45 | www.ela-Chaniá.gr | Moderate*

THE FAMOUS
From mid-July until the beginning of September daily, otherwise during weekends – live Greek dance music. *From 10pm | Pl. Santriváni*

INSIDER TIP KRÍTI ●
Original and simple *ouzerí* behind the Arsenals where Cretan *lýra* players perform for a mixed audience. Simple fare and authentic music. *Daily from about 8pm | Odós Kallergón 22 | Budget*

WHERE TO STAY

AMPHORA

20 rooms (one with a four-poster bed), some with a kitchenette in a house dating back to the 14th century. Decorated with antiques. *Párodos Theotokopúlu 20 | tel. 28 21 09 32 24 | www.amphora.gr | Moderate*

BELMONDO

Stylish old town hotel in the harbour. The wooden facade harks back to the Ottoman Empire and the furniture to the Venetian era. Very modern technology. *8 rooms | Odós Zambéliu 10 | tel. 28 21 03 62 16 | www.belmondohotel.com | Moderate–Expensive*

CASA DELFINO

20 tastefully decorated studios with air-conditioning and kitchenettes in a 17th century manor house with an interior court-yard and roof terrace for guests. *Odós Theofánus 9 | tel. 28 21 09 30 98 | www.casadelfino.com | Expensive*

KASTELI

These six studios and apartments (accommodating up to six people each) are situated in the old town. Decorated with light wood and Cretan tapestry some of them are in a lovely courtyard and they all have an authentic Chaniá atmosphere. *Odós Kanaváro 39 | tel. 28 21 05 70 57 | www.kastelistudios-crete.com | Moderate*

INSIDER TIP PALAZZO

This old town house with wooden floors and marble baths is decorated in the Cretan style and has a pretty roof garden. The 11 air-conditioned apartments are over 40 m² (430 ft²) with separate living rooms and bedrooms. *Odós Theotokópulu*

Pleasant ritual: evening stroll past the tavernas on Chaniá's harbour

*54 | tel. 28 21 09 32 27 | www.palazzohotel.
gr | Moderate*

MUNICIPAL TOURIST INFORMATION
*Odós Milonogiánni 53 (town hall) | tel.
28 21 34 16 65 | www.chania.gr*
Mid June–Sept additional info at the kiosk
on the southern side of the municipal
market and on the northern side of the
Janissary Mosque.

**SOCIETY FOR THE PROTECTION OF
SEA TURTLES** ☺
Throughout the summer volunteers for
the Greek Society for the Protection of Sea
Turtles operate an information stand on
the promenade in front of the Janissary
Mosque. Here you can learn more about
the behaviour and the Cretan nesting
beaches of the loggerhead turtles, as well
as how you as a holidaymaker can con-
tribute to their conservation.

WHERE TO GO

AGÍA ROUMÉLI
(135 E6) *(Ø C4)*
The ruins of a Turkish castle tower over
this southern coast town at the end of the
Samariá Gorge. Here you will find tavernas and guest houses. A swim at the pebbled beach is the perfect end to a walk
through the gorge. During peak seasons,
Agía Rouméli is connected to Chóra Sfakíon
and Paleochóra by a daily boat, there is
no road.

AKROTÍRI PENINSULA ⭐
(136 A–B 1–2) *(Ø D–E 1–2)*
The city's airport is situated on this peninsula east of Chaniá, as well as a Nato
missile launching base. In the 500 m high
mountains to the north, the 17th century
monastery *Agía Triáda* (where monks still

The abandoned Katholikó
monastery in Akrotíri

reside) has been restored in the traditional style and is well worth a visit. *(Daily
7.30am–2pm and 5–7pm)*, and *Guvernétu*
from the 16th century *(Sun 5–11am and
5–8pm, Mon, Tue, Thu, Sat 10am–1pm
and 5–8pm, Oct–Easter 4–6pm, closed
Mon and Fri)*.
From Guvernétu you can take a 30 minute
hike down to the cave church *Panagía*,
the stalactite cave *Jéro Spíleo* and to the
abandoned *Katholikó* monastery. *Round
trip about 50–60 km (30–37 mi)*.

ALMIRÍDA (136 B2) (*m E3*)

On the western outskirts of this quiet resort with its sandy beaches are the remains of a mosaic floor from an early Christian basilica. *24 km (15 mi)*

A particularly scenic drive takes you through the old villages of *Pláka*, *Drápanas* and *Kefalás* to *Georgioúpoli*. You should make a pit stop in ● *Kókkino Chorió*, where a well known *glass blower* produces practical and decorative items from recycled glass. *20 km (13 mi)*

ÁPTERA ☭ (136 B2) (*m D2*)

The ruins of a once mighty Greco-Roman city can be found on this nearly 200 m (764 ft) high mountain plateau with a beautiful view of the Soúda Bay. Explore the remains of the city wall, various temples and cisterns, a theatre and a medieval monastery as well as a Turkish castle *(ruins Tue–Sun 8.30am–3pm | admission free | castle freely accessible at all times). 16 km (10 mi)*

CHÓRA SFAKÍON
(136 B5) (*m D4*)

The picturesque main town of Sfakiá, situated in a bay with white-washed houses and narrow alleys, is only crowded with holidaymakers in the early afternoon. After the hike through the Samariá Gorge and the boat trip from Agía Rouméli they board their buses here which will take them through dozens of hairpin bends in the direction of the north coast.

Glikánera is an especially beautiful beach where fresh and saltwater meet. *Kaíkis* depart daily from 10am from the old port and return at 5pm.

If you prefer peace and quiet and can handle the heat (it gets very hot here) you should stay at *Stavris (34 rooms | tel. 28 25 09 12 20 | www.hotelstavris-chora-sfakion. com | Moderate)* above the port or in the *Ilingas Beach Hotel*, 2000 m away on a mostly deserted pebble beach *(16 rooms | tel. 28 25 09 12 39 | www.ilingas.sfakia-kreta.gr/en | Budget). 73 km (45 mi)*

CHRISOSKALÍTISSA MONASTERY ★
(134 A5) (*m A4*)

Alone on a low cliff above the ocean is a modern looking small, white monastery. It has been abandoned many times in its turbulent history; in 1944 Germans demolished many of its buildings. Behind the monastery, a number of new houses have been built over the last few decades, where there are rooms for rent. There is now a bus service in the summer from Chaniá and Kissámos. *73 km (45 mi)*

ELAFONÍSI ★ (134 A5) (*m A4*)

5 km (3 mi) south of Chrisoskalítissa is a South Sea-style beach upstream from the small island of Elafonísi. During the summer it is connected to the Cretan mainland

VENDETTAS & WEAPONS

Vendettas have been outlawed in Sfakiá for more than 30 years. But in Sfakiá the men are as reluctant as the rest of Crete to give up their weapons. The holes in most Cretan road signs are due to target practice and sometimes during weddings salvos of gunshots are fired off. In her novel *Shadow Wedding*, Ioanna Karystianis describes what vendettas meant in Sfakiá in 1972, when a young groom has to kill his father's murderer.

by a sand bank, giving the sea the appearance of a lagoon with shimmering green and blue hues. The shore falls off gently making it very child friendly; shade is provided by umbrellas. There are also some snack bars and tavernas and during summer you can also take a boat trip from Paleochóra to Elafonísi. *78 km (48 mi)*

very flat and ideal for small children. A great place to stay is INSIDER TIP *Maria's Apartments* on the beach next to an old windmill, which can be rented as a holiday home *(17 rooms | tel. 28 25 09 21 59 | Budget)*. The municipal bus connects Frangokastéllo once daily with Chóra Sfakíon and Plakiás. *80 km (50 mi)*

With mountains as the backdrop and views of the sea – Frangokastéllo fortress ruins

FRANGOKASTÉLLO ✕
(136 B–C5) (*Ø E4–5*)

At the edge of a wide coastal plain with the White Mountains as backdrop, the Venetians built (in 1371) a small castle right on the water. Its crenulated walls with the Venetian coat of arms on the south portal still stands today, but only the ruins are left of the interior walls.

At the foot of the castle lies a long, broad stretch of sandy beach. The shoreline is

GEORGIOÚPOLI
(136 C3) (*Ø E3*)

This town was named after the high commissioner Prince George who was elected after the Turks left Crete. Tall eucalyptus trees line the beautiful platía with its many cafés, the sandy beach stretches for miles and the small river port north of the town is full of atmosphere. A short walk from the platía towards the beach is the shop ☺ *Braoudakis*. Here you can buy organic products from the region: olives and olive oil, *raki* and honey, jams and much more. You are also welcome to sample the products. At the beginning of the western beach, the *Beach Bar Tropicana* with its exotic pagoda roof welcomes you. During the peak season the young waiters and waitresses host a typical *Cretan evening.* A few steps further, a second river mouth runs into the sea. Here, the taverna *Perastikos (daily from 10am | Budget)* offers simple food, coffee and drinks right on the river bank. Guests can even try their hand at luring turtles or eels with bread. Cretan hospitality is very much alive at Stélios and Perséfoni's INSIDER TIP guest house *Stélios Kokolákis* in the eastern centre *(12 rooms | tel. 28 25 06 13 08 | Budget)*. If you prefer a self-catering studio, the *Riverhouse* approx. 300 m outside of town is ideal. This small double-storey house, with a pool and pool bar, belongs to an English speaking family. Some studios have enough room for a family with two children *(16 rooms | on the road to Vámos | tel. 28 25 06 11 41 | www.riverhouse.gr | Budget)*. *40 km (24 mi)*

ÍMBROS GORGE (136 B5) (𝄞 E4)

One of the easiest gorge hikes in Crete starts in *Ímbros,* a town at the southern edge of the Askífou Plateau. It takes about three hours to get to the town of *Komitádes,* where you can then take the bus in the early afternoon on to *Chóra Sfakíon.* There the best taverna is the *Ostría,* which also rents out rooms *(tel. 28 25 09 13 09 | Budget).* The gorge is almost as narrow as the Samariá Gorge and has rock faces 40 to 50 m (130 to 160 ft) high *(entrance 2 euros). 57 km (35 mi)*

INSIDER TIP IRÍNI GORGE
(135 D5) (𝄞 B4)

The Iríni Gorge is just as impressive as the Samariá Gorge but is not as well known.

The rock faces soar hundreds of metres high and many parts of the gorge are covered in forest and huge boulders lie in the summer dry river bed. The hike starts at the southern edge of the village of *Agía Iríni* on the road from Chaniá to Soúgia. A small forest restaurant is at the entrance. The gorge ends after 7 km (4 mi) at a simple little INSIDER TIP *Taverna Oásis (Budget),* which fits in perfectly with the landscape. The selection is limited but the food authentic. From here a road continues for 5 km (3 mi) to Soúgia *(taxi booking tel. 28 23 05 14 84 or tel. 28 23 05 14 85). 56 km (34 mi)*

KISSÁMOS
(134 B3) (𝄞 A2)

The most western city of the island (pop. 3000) is still largely untouched by tourism. It lies on a lovely bay flanked by two peninsulas and has both pebbled and

sandy beaches. Good accommodation available at *Stavroúla Palace (some 50 m west of the beach promenade | tel. 28 22 02 23 15 | Budget).*

A boat trip to the Venetian island fortress *Gramvoúsa* followed by a swim at the sandy beach of *Bálos afterwards (approx. 25 euros | info tel. 28 22 02 43 44 | www. gramvousa.com)* and a visit to the new *Archaeological Museum* with its beautiful floor mosaics *(Tue–Sun 8.30am–3pm | admission free | Pl. El. Venizélou)* is a must. *42 km (26 mi)*

KOURNÁS LAKE
(136 C4) (*Ɱ E3*)

Crete's largest lake is surrounded by mountains and is situated close to the bay of Georgioúpoli. Here you can swim or ride on paddle boats or spend time at one of the several tavernas are situated on the shore. *37 km (23 mi)*

LOUTRÓ ⭐ (136 A5) (*Ɱ D4*)

A little hamlet on the southern coast of the island that can only be reached by boat from Paleochóra or Chóra Sfakíon. Here you can dive from cliffs into the small bay and accommodation is available at the INSIDER TIP Hotel *Pórto Loutró*, where a British/Greek couple not only ensure peace and quiet (no mobile phones allowed), but also a friendly British atmosphere as well as near perfect cleanliness *(42 rooms/studios | tel. 28 25 09 14 33 | www.hotelportoloutro.com | Moderate). 73 km (45 mi)*

MÁLEME (125 D3) (*Ɱ C2*)

This former British airfield was one of the main targets of the Germans during the German invasion in 1941. There is a memorial to the airmen of 30 and 33 Squadrons in the cemetery on the fiercely contested Hill 107. *19 km (11¾ mi)*

A picture-perfect bay – Loutró is only accessible by boat

MILIÁ ☺ ●

(134 B4) (🗺 A3)

In 1982 a few former citizens of the dilapidated mountain village of Miliá decided to renovate the houses as holiday homes and to make them the core of an eco-project that also included agriculture and forestry. This completely car-free village has 13 natural stone houses with Cretan interiors which are now available as rentals. Water is heated by the sun, candles and oil lamps are used for light. The drinking water comes from a nearby spring and in the village taverna uses only locally produced organic products. *(tel. 28 21 04 67 74 | www.milia.gr | Moderate)*. *60 km (37 mi)*

OMALÓS PLATEAU

(135 D5) (🗺 C3–4)

This 1050 m (3444 ft) high plateau covers about 6000 acres and serves as a grazing area for goats and sheep. The descent into the Samariá Gorge starts at *Xylóskala* at its southern end. The hotel *Exari* in the village of *Omalós* is a good option to eat and to stay *(24 rooms | tel. 28 21 06 71 80 | www.exari.gr | Budget)*. This way INSIDER TIP▶ you will be first at the gorge in the morning. *37 km (23 mi)*

PALEOCHÓRA

(134 B6) (🗺 B4)

The citizens of this once isolated coastal village used to call it 'The bride of the Libyan Sea'. The village is now a popular resort with pebbled and sandy beaches. There are no big hotels so visitors stay in small guest houses and apartments. The whole village centre turns into a large taverna at night. Opposite the village church the permanent exhibition *The Acritans of Europe* shows the similarities between the Byzantine and the Western heroes' sagas *(Mon–Fri 10am–1pm| admission free)*. Further down the road you will find the castle grounds of *Kástro Sélino* dating from Venetian times, overgrown with wild herbs, its grounds reach down to the end of the peninsula. From the castle you can see to Gavdos, the southernmost island of Europe, and a popular meeting place at sundown.

Stay right on the beach at the hotel *Villa Marise (16 rooms | tel. 28 23 04 11 62 | www.villamarise.com | Moderate)*. In the evenings everyone meets at the open air cinema (English films are shown from 10pm) or in the open air dance club *Paleochóra Club* near the campground right next to the sea. *77 km (47 mi)*

POLIRRINÍA

(134 B3) (🗺 A2–3)

About ten minutes walk above the modern village of Polirrinía are the ☆ ruins of the ancient city of Polirrinía. The pathway starts at the Byzantine church *Ágii Patéres*, with its tombstones built into the exterior walls. Wall and building remains are loosely strewn across the wild countryside where yellow fennel blooms during spring. The views and the peace are memorable *(admission free to grounds, church closed)*. *53 km (33 mi)*

SFAKIÁ PLATEAU (136 B5) (🗺 D4)

Sfakiá and Lassíthi in the east of Crete are two of the island's most densely populated plateaus. Once a wild and inaccessible area, the Turks were never able to overthrow its citizens – something that they are still very proud of today. The Sfakiots farm cattle, potatoes, grapes, fruit and walnuts. In the Sfakiá village tavernas they serve *Sfakiániés píttes* a local speciality which is a pancake filled with honey and goat's cheese. *50 km (30 mi)*

SOÚGIA (134 C6) (🗺 B4)

This little hamlet on the south coast has long pebble beaches with a few caves that offer lovely shade. The village church Ágios Pantelímonas has retained its early Christian mosaic floor which depicts two peacocks and a deer. A good accommodation option is the guest house *El Greco*, which is a few hundred metres from the sea in the north-western edge of the village *(15 rooms | tel. 28 23 05 10 26 | www.sougia.info | Budget)*. 70 km (43 mi)

(Vámos SA | tel. 28 25 02 32 51 | www. vamossa.gr | Moderate). Good Cretan food can be enjoyed in the taverna *I Stérna tou Bloumósifis* in the main road *(Moderate)*.

Also worth a visit is the neighbouring village of *Gavalochóri* with its modern *Folk Museum (Mon–Sat 9am–7pm, Sun 10am–1.30pm and 5–7pm | 2 euros)*. Especially idyllic is the half hour **INSIDER TIP** walk to

Bizarre rocks on Soúgia beach – as yet unspoiled by mass tourism

VÁMOS ★ ● (136 B3) *(൜ E3)*

Vámos (pop. 650) is situated in between vineyards and is the main town of the rural (and relatively undiscovered) Apokóronas region. Most of the houses date back to the 19th century and some two dozen of them can be rented as holiday homes

the neighbouring village *Douliana* along a dry river bed which leads to a stone chapel *Ágios Ioánnis*. You can also take a guided hike through the region with *Faragi Tours* in Vámos *(tel. 28 25 02 28 27, mobile 69 42 60 96 79 | www.faragitours. com)*. 22 km (13 mi)#

RÉTHIMNO

Réthimno, despite being Crete's third largest city, has a sense of tranquility. The old town is almost as well preserved as that of Chaniá's but the houses are more modest and the harbour smaller. Réthimno does not have the hectic pace of the capital Iráklio because traffic is mostly banned from the old town. No car will interrupt your view of the Venetian harbour when you sit down to enjoy some fish. Most of the old town houses are still owned by the original families.

The whole province has the same feel as the city. It is situated between the two massifs of the White Mountains and the Psilorítis, wide valleys lead from the north

to the south coast with its seaside resorts of Plakiás and Agía Galini. These two places are a nice middle ground. Although they attract many tourists, these tourists do not stay in the large hotels, but in the small hotels, flats and guest houses.

The long sandy beaches east of Réthimno are a paradise for water sport fanatics and the beautiful countryside is perfect for hikes and mountain bike trips for the whole family. From Réthimno, Plakiás and Agía Galini there are also a number of boats to take tourists out to the isolated beaches of the area. If you are looking for peace, you will find it here. The coast between Agía Galini and the palm canyon of

Photo: Venetian harbour in Réthimno

Historical flair: here you can combine sun-bathing with journeys of discovery along the enchanted paths of the past

Préveli is not called Crete's yoga coast for nothing – many believe that the earth's forces are particularly strong here.

RÉTHIMNO

MAP INSIDE BACK COVER
(137 D–E3) (𝄞 F3) **Réthimno (pop. 28,000)** is a friendly, atmospheric little town. Its old town area is in good condition with lot of minarets and mosques, narrow alleys and wide squares, houses with typical Turkish wooden bays and parts of the city wall still intact.

The old town takes up a peninsula, with a massive fortress at the tip. The modern harbour basin is situated on its south-eastern side, followed by the picturesque Venetian harbour. A 12 km (7 mi) long

CITY **WHERE TO START**
Platía Tésseron Mártiron:
Buses travelling from Iráklio and
Chaniá stop directly at the edge of
the old town. South of this platía
you will find a metered car park
which offers the best parking spot.

sandy beach stretches from the harbour
pier. This stretch of beach continues to be
developed with hotels, guest houses and
apartments. Behind the city wall, which
is now marked by a main road, lies the
sprawling new town.

Réthimno is dominated by holidaymakers
keen to spend time in the hotels close to
the beach and only come in the town to
eat or shop, as well as those who prefer
to stay in the historic old town in cosy
guest houses or the modern urban hotels.
For both types, the city has its attraction.
Réthimno also has a number of cultural
activities. The University of Crete, has a
campus here (as well as in Iráklio and
Chaniá) and it is also home to the
Philosophy Faculty so the city is seen as
the intellectual centre of the island.
Réthimno also has a theatre, a philhar-
monic society and an adult education
college exclusively for women. During the
summer months there are guest performances by local and foreign music and
theatre groups.

The peninsula of Réthimno was probably
only settled in the late Minoan era. The
city was called Rhythymna and was con-

An impressive site: the massive fortress walls of the Venetian Fortézza

sidered by the Venetians to be the island's most important city after Iráklio and Chaniá. In 1645, 24 years before Iráklio, Réthimno was conquered by the Turks.

SIGHTSEEING

ARCHAEOLOGICAL MUSEUM

Objects from the Stone Age to the Venetian era are exhibited in what was once a Turkish prison. Especially interesting are the Egyptian exhibits, like the small brass statue of the goddess Isis (testimony to the sea trade with Egypt) as well as the coin collection and the Roman bronze figure of a warrior that was found in a shipwreck at Agía Galini. The late-Minoan warrior helmet with boar teeth sewn on with leather is also noteworthy. *Tue–Sun 8.30am–3pm | entrance 3 euros | opposite the entrance to the Fortézza*

FORTÉZZA ★ ⚹

Only the exterior walls of this 16th century Venetian castle still remain. Behind them in a wild and untamed landscape are the ruins of different buildings; a Christian chapel, a mosque and a number of cisterns. During the summer it is the venue for cultural events held under the night sky. *May–Oct daily 9am–7pm, in winter as required | entrance 3 euros | entrance at the eastern side*

KANAKÁKIS GALLERY

Paintings by 20th century Greek artists are on display along with temporary exhibitions of contemporary art. *Tue–Fri 9am–2pm, Wed also 5–9pm, Sat/Sun 10am–3pm | entrance 3 euros | Odós Chimáras/Odós Melissínu*

LOGGIA ★

Once a meeting place where Venetian nobles discussed politics, it has been beautifully restored and today serves as an official museum shop, where copies of museum pieces from all over Greece are sold. *Daily 8am–4pm | Odós Arkadíu 220*

KARA MUSSA PASCHA MOSQUE

A small mosque with the remains of early paintings and old Turkish tombs. *Odós Arkadíu/Ecke Odós Viktóros Ugó*

TIS NERANTZE MOSQUE

The three domes and the 18th century minaret can be seen from a distance. Today it is home to a music school. *Platía Títus Peticháki*

RIMÓNDI FOUNTAIN

This elegant Venetian fountain from 1623 has survived along with many other old Turkish fountains in the centre of the old town. Three lion heads between four slender columns sprout water into the fountain. It was originally covered by a dome, which has fallen prey to street expansions. *Platía Títu Peticháki*

★ **Fortézza**
Summer concerts take place in the picturesque castle ruins with panoramic views → p. 49

★ **Loggia**
Buy souvenirs that can transform your home into a Greek museum → p. 49

★ **Venetian harbour**
Crete's most beautiful harbour basin, lined with cafés and seafood tavernas → p. 50

★ **Arkádi Monastery**
This famous island monastery is a national shrine → p. 55

MARCO POLO HIGHLIGHTS

CITY PARK

In the green oasis on the border between the old town and the modern town of Réthimno, a few Cretan wild goats live in small enclosure next to a children's play ground. A small outdoor self-service cafeteria *(Budget)* provides refreshments. *From sunrise to sunset | admission free | Platía Tésseron Mártiron*

BEACH PROMENADE

A lovely 45 minute (approx.) evening walk takes you from the bus station along the beach promenade to the fortress up to the Venetian harbour with numerous cafés along the way.

VENETIAN HARBOUR ★

Venetian ships once dropped anchor here where today there are only yachts and fishing boats. The Venetians built the breakwater, the Ottomans built the lighthouse and the beautiful houses (now under a preservation order) with their

balconies and portals also date back to this time. On the facades of some of these houses, weathered coats of arms are still visible. The chairs and tables of fish tavernas take up most of the space in front of these houses – leaving little space for passers-by.

HISTORICAL & FOLK ART MUSEUM

The way of life and work of Cretans during the 18th and 19th century is documented here. *Mon–Sat 10am–2.30pm | entrance 4 euros | Odós Vernádu 28–30*

FOOD & DRINK

INSIDER TIP KNOSSÓS

One of the oldest tavernas in the Venetian harbour has been owned by the same family for more than 50 years. Mother is the chef, who ensures the quality of the food while daughter Maria and son Stávros ensure excellent and friendly service. *Daily from noon | Moderate*

In Réthimno's old town you can shop late into the night

OUSÍES ●

Typical *rakádiko* with many Cretan dishes, some of which have been refined. Also serving dishes from other islands like haloumi (a goat's cheese from Cypress) served with mint sauce. *Daily from noon | Odós Vernádu 20 | tel. 28 31 05 66 43 | Moderate*

LA RENZO

Sophisticated restaurant in a 500-year old vaulted cellar. Greek and international dishes. The speciality of the house is *souvlaki* made with kid goat and Cretan lamb with honey. The Australian owner Christina guarantees excellent steaks. Her husband Manolis loves excellent Greek wines and is happy to discuss them in English. *Daily 6pm–1am | Odós Radamanthíu 9 | Expensive*

LEMON TREE GARDEN

A taverna aimed at tourists and set in a lemon tree garden. In order for guests to also be able to sample Cretan cuisine, a *meze* with 13 dishes is also available *(approx. 14 euros)* and there is also a *Cretan menu (approx. 18 euros). Daily from noon | Odós Ethn. Antistáseos 100 | Moderate*

SHOPPING

SHOPPING STREETS

The beautiful alley *Odós Arkadíu* in the old town is Réthimno's main shopping street. The locals also buy their shoes and clothes here. Souvenir shops can be found in *Ethnikís Antistásseos, Súlion* and *Paleológou* streets and the best Greek delicacies at *Avlí* in *Armanpatzóglou 40 (Arabatzóglou).*

MARKETS

Thursdays near the marina, Saturdays near to the bus terminal. Fruit, vegetables, textiles and small technical appliances from the Far East are mostly on offer. *7am–1pm*

SPORTS & LEISURE

The 16 km (10 mi) beach that stretches from the harbour to the east is open for swimming. At most of the big hotels, water sports equipment is available, from paddle boats to waterskis, windsurfers and paragliders. The *Atlantis Dive Centre* on *Aquila Rithýmna beach* in Ádele caters for divers as does the *Grecotel Club Marina Palace* in Panórmo *(tel. 28 31 07 16 40 | www.atlantis-creta.com)*.

INSIDER TIP Guided hikes and bicycle tours in the area are undertaken in English by Manólis Kagiannákis including sunset mountain hikes and gorge hikes. *(Nature & Adventure | Odós K. Gikampudáki 14 | tel. 28 31 05 41 35 | www.nat-adv.gr)*.

ENTERTAINMENT

ASTÉRIA ●

Open air cinema and bar underneath the Venetian fortress walls. *Odós Melisínu/ Ecke Odós Smírnis | entrance 7 euros*

O GUNÁS

Original old town taverna where the proprietor's sons plays the *lýra* from 10pm. Simple fare (like crêpes) and authentic Cretan music. *Odós P. Koronéu 4–6*

LIVINGROOM

This is the trendiest bar on the promenade and the place to see and be seen. It serves everything the young Greek heart desires, from Greek coffee to French Champagne as well as 18 different Greek

Excursion boats depart daily from Agía Galíni to the surrounding beaches

wines per glass and ice cream sundaes. In typical Cretan fashion, guests receive a thirst quenching glass of water before they order. *Odós El. Venizélou 5*

ODÓS VERNÁRDOU

In the narrow alleyways of the old town the traditional rakádika are all crammed in alongside each other. Here the young and the old enjoy many Cretan specialities and prefer to order *rakí* as a drink. Live music is also played in certain venues, from Cretan *lýra* to Greek rock.

WHERE TO STAY

AQUILA RITHÝMNA BEACH

One of the best organised hotels with bungalows, restaurants, saltwater and

freshwater pools, an indoor pool, sport and other activities. 7 km (4¼ mi) east of Réthimno on the beach. *520 rooms | Ádele | tel. 28 31 07 10 02 | www.aquila hotels.com | Expensive*

FORTÉZZA

Completely renovated house with a pool, which fits in perfectly with the old town, just beneath the fortress. Ideal for tourists travelling with rental cars for stop-over accommodation, due to their free private car park. *54 rooms | Odós Melisínu 16 | tel. 28 31 05 55 51 | www.fortezza.gr | Moderate*

INSIDER TIP OLGA'S PENSION

Lovely old-fashioned guest house in the old town, somewhat chaotic, proprietor speaks good English, beautiful roof garden. A quaint meeting place for travellers! *8 rooms | tel. 28 31 05 32 06 | Odós Soulioú 57 | Budget*

PALAZZO VECCHIO

Hotel in a Venetian palace dating from the 15th century. A small pool in the courtyard and a terrace with deckchairs and umbrellas on the roof. *25 apartments | Odós Melissínou/corner of Platía Iróon Politechníu | tel. 28 31 03 53 51 | www.palazzovecchio.gr | Expensive*

INFORMATION

TOURIST INFORMATION

Prokiméa Elefthérios Venizélou | tel. 28 31 02 91 48 | www.rethymnon.gr

WHERE TO GO

AGÍA GALÍNI
(138 B4) *(𝟭 H5)*

This densely built village stretches from the harbour – with its modern memorial to Daedalos and Icarus – about 300 m inland into a narrow valley. Its few streets

Arkádi Monastery where silence and peace reign today – once the scene of bloody battles

are lined with bars and restaurants and its modern houses are mainly built on the mountain slopes. The village has its own beach 200 m north of the harbour and a number of boats also leave daily to beaches in the surrounding area. Agía Galini is ideal for tourists who love the beach during the day and a vibrant nightlife in the evening. *55 km (34 mi)*

ARGIROÚPOLI
(136 C4) *(ⓜ F4)*

A beautiful mosaic from Roman times has survived in the old part of this mountain village. At the village gate across the main church you can obtain free village maps in a little shop that sells 😊 **INSIDER TIP** cosmetics made from avocados cultivated in the area. Since 2011, natural products made from carob are also sold.

At the lower village edge, waterfalls bubble from a strong spring which supplies Réthimno with its drinking water. Various forest tavernas offer fresh trout. A three minute walk towards Káto Póros, you will find many excavated Roman graves next to the *Pénde Párthenon chapel*. Good accommodation is available in the *Láppa Apartments* above the square and below the main road. The proprietor is also happy to transport guests to the starting point for hikes and excursions in his off-road vehicle *(7 rooms | tel. 28 31 08 11 44 | www.lappa.georgioupolis-creta.org/ home/ | Budget). 21 km (13 mi)*

ASÓMATOS
(137 D5) *(ⓜ F4)*

The village priest Michális Georgioulákis (1921–2008) always did everything differ-

with open fireplaces out in the middle of nature. There is a small pool, an excellent Cretan restaurant and even horses to ride. As part of their ⏱ eco-tourism offer, you can take part in agricultural activities such as cheese-making; go on botanical walks or on bird-watching tours *(20 apartments | follow signposts in the town | tel. 28 34 06 16 11 | www.enagron.gr and www.guestinn. gr | Moderate)*. 43 km (26 mi)

ARKÁDI MONASTERY ★
(137 F4) (*ØØ G4*)

This fortified monastery on a 500 m (1500 ft) high mountain plateau is Crete's national shrine, once a terrible scene of rebellion against the Ottoman rule. The small *museum* exhibits portraits of the participants and other memorabilia. The remains of the victims can be seen in the ossuary opposite the entrance. The gunpowder room, in which the women and children blew themselves up in 1866 in order to escape the Turks, has not been restored. The monastery church facade with its mixture of Renaissance and baroque elements has been restored *(open daily | entrance 2 euros)*. 23 km (14 mi)

MARGARÍTES ●
(138 B2) (*ØØ H3*)

Crete's best known potters' village is situated on a green hill. Before the war approx. 50 potters produced large storage vessels – called *píthoi* – which date back to Minoan times. Nowadays the village has been settled by young artisans and ceramic artists who produce sophisticated souvenirs. The *píthoi* are now only manufactured in the last potter's workshop at the edge of the village on the road leading to Eléftherna. The two 🌿 *taverna (Budget)* on the small village square serve Cretan specials and cold draft beer under large mulberry trees, with lovely views of the coast and the ocean. 27 km (16 mi)

ently and as such his **INSIDER TIP** *village museum (daily 10am–3pm | entrance 3 euros)* is quite unique. On display is everything that he has collected from surrounding villages, bought at flea markets or inherited over the past 60 years. His English speaking daughter-in-law Sísi leads tours through this bizarre collection and she also runs an isolated 🌿 guest house *Farági* that has fantastic views *(4 rooms | tel. 28 32 03 11 58 | Budget)*. 30 km (18½ mi)

AXÓS
(138 C2) (*ØØ J4*)

This unspoiled mountain village offers the ⏱ **INSIDER TIP** *Hotel Enágron* for an interesting stay. Here you will stay in a little village that has been built in the Cretan style, in traditionally furnished studios

MELIDÓNI CAVE
(138 B1) (*H3*)

This cave is well signposted from the coastal motorway and like the Arkádi Monastery it recalls the Greek resistance to Turkish rule. In 1824, 340 Greek women and children and 30 Cretan resistance fighters hid in this cave. They died from smoke inhalation from a fire set by the Turks. A sarcophagus in the dramatically lit cave holds their remains *(daily 9am–6*

The Préveli Gorge flows into a turquoise blue sea

pm | 3 euros). The ● INSIDER TIP *Paráskis olive oil factory* is situated at the edge of the village where approx. 400 t of olive oil is pressed every winter. The owner's wife Ioánna Paraskáki guides visitors around and explains the process in English *(open during the day | admission free)*. *31 km (19 mi)*

PLAKIÁS
(137 D5) (*F4*)

Plakiás together with mountain villages *Mýrthios* and *Sellía* form a tourism unit. Surrounded by olive groves the 800 m (2600 ft) long sandy beach of Plakiás is great for swimming (nudist beach in the east), and in the west you can sit at tavernas at the water's edge. Tourists stay in small guest houses and apartments, most of which are situated in quiet olive groves. Marked walking trails lead to the ruins of a 100-year old watermill and to the villages of Mýrthios and Sellía, where there is also accommodation. Travel agents offer guided walks through the gorges as well as mountain bikes tours (info: *www.plakias.net*). Away from the bustle at the eastern end of the beach you can stay at the *Hotel Plakias Bay (tel. 28 23 03 12 15 | www.plakiasbay. com | Moderate), a* chic hot spot is *Fame* in the centre of the promenade *(Moderate)*. *40 km (24 mi)*

PRÉVELI
(137 D–E6) (*F5*)

Préveli has three sights worth visiting: a monastery, the romantic ruins of a monastery and a palm tree gorge. Coming from the main road, walk about 2000 m to the 19th century bridge, a further 600 m below the road are the ruins of the *Káto Préveli Monastery*. The road ends 3.2 km (2 mi) further at the *Piso Préveli Monastery (25 March–May daily 8am–7pm, June–Oct Mon–Sat 8am–1.30pm* and 3.30–7.30pm, Sun 8am–7.30pm | entrance 3 euros). In 1941, the monks hid British soldiers until they could be picked up by submarines. The *monastery museum* houses valuable icons. There are three ways to reach the gorge: a 7 km (4 mi) unsurfaced track leads you from the Turkish bridge to a neighbouring rocky cove, from where you can take a boat taxi or take a 10 minute walk to Préveli beach. You can also reach it by boat from Agía Galíni und Plakiás during the summer. A steep path leads down below the road between Káto and Píso Préveli and takes about in about 30 minutes to get to the beach.

At the beach a cold river flows into the sea from the Kourtaliátiko Gorge, a narrow canyon overgrown by palm trees. A devastating fire caused huge damage in 2010 from which the palms are slowly recuperating. You can head upstream as far as possible but you will have to clamber over rapids and rocks, wade through knee high or chest high water and at certain places you even have to swim. *37 km (23 mi)*

SPÍLI
(137 E5) (*ill G4*)

A mountain village on the main road from Réthimno to Agía Galini and Festós that is the seat of a Greek Orthodox seminary. Excursion buses stop here during the day, but in the evening there are usually only locals. In the *Yannis* taverna in the centre, you can enjoy gyros and yoghurt with walnuts or vegetables fresh from the taverna garden *(Budget)*. They also have good private rooms *(Budget)* on offer. Worth seeing is the *Venetian fountain* with lion heads in the main road which is also surrounded by modern cafés and cocktail bars. *30 km (18½ mi)*

BOOKS & FILMS

▶ **Zorba the Greek** – A Cretan classic (both book and film) written by Níkos Kazantzákis and directed by Michael Cacoyanni in 1964 with Anthony Quinn, Alan Bates and Irene Pappas in the lead roles.

▶ **Freedom or Death** – This novel by Kazantzákis has as its backdrop the Cretan rebellion against Ottoman rule and is set in 19th century Iráklio.

▶ **The Island** – This historical novel by award-winning author Victoria Hislop is set on the former leper colony of Spinalónga, an island off the Cretan coast.

▶ **The Chronicle of a Town** – This book by Pantélis Prevelákis is only available in Crete. It describes the author's childhood memories and the slow decline of his hometown Réthimno during the first third of the 20th century.

▶ **The Greek Passion** – Set in 1948 Nikos Kazantzakis tells the story of a village that is rehearsing the Passion and is suddenly confronted by a group of refugees driven from their homes by the Turks.

▶ **He Who Must Die** – A 1956 film directed by Jules Dassin based on the novel *Christ Recrucified* by Níkos Kazantzákis and filmed on Crete.

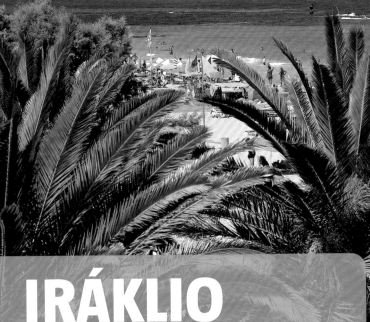

IRÁKLIO

Iraklio is the centre of Cretan life. A quarter of the islands inhabitants live here. In Minoan times this metropolis was important due to its central location and proximity to Knossós and Festós.

The more alternative Mátala, on the other hand, is in contrast to northern resorts like Chersónisos and Mália which have the most hotel rooms on the island.

the island's largest city – vibrant Iráklio (pop. 131,000) – which is also where the majority of tourist first arrive.

IRÁKLIO

MAP INSIDE BACK COVER
(139 E–F2) *(∅ K–L3)* **To understand modern Crete, you must first visit**

WHERE TO START?
Venetian harbour: to avoid the problem of finding parking in Iráklio, it is best to go there by bus. If you arrive by car, park along the shore at the commercial port (mostly free) where ferries and cruise liners drop anchor, then walk in a westerly direction for 5–15 minutes to the Venetian harbour in the old town.

Photo: Mália beach

The heartbeat of the island: the ancient centre of the Minoan world has evolved into an extremely popular holiday destination

The capital city which sprawls along the coast has undergone a remarkable transformation. Today you can sit and watch fishing boats and ferries from the Venetian harbour or from trendy café terraces. Modern cafés have transformed its squares and streets into bustling open air lounges. Follow a market browse with a Greek espresso by the Venetian fountain before heading out to explore some museums and churches or spend the day doing some relaxed shopping in the extensive pedestrian zone and then enjoy some delicious Cretan fare in a local restaurant.

SIGHTSEEING

ÁGIOS MÁRKOS CHURCH

The oldest Venetian church built in 1239 (close to the Morosini Fountain) today

The beautiful frescoes in Iráklio's Ágios Minás cathedral are from more recent times

hosts concerts and exhibitions. The monolithic pillars of the basilica date back to ancient times. *Opening times differ | admission free | Odós 25 Avgústu*

ÁGIOS MINÁS CHURCH

The cathedral of Iráklio built 1862–95 can house 8000 people. The fantastic frescoes and decorations date back to the 1960s. *Mostly open during the day | admission free | Platia Agía Ekaterinis*

ÁGIOS TÍTOS CHURCH

The relic of Saint Titus' skull is housed in this church which was converted from a mosque to a church in 1923. Títus was a scholar of the apostle Paul and the island's first bishop. *Daily 7am–noon and 5–8pm | admission free | Odós 25 Avgústu*

ARCHAEOLOGICAL MUSEUM ★

No other museum in the world has more items from the Minoan era and for this reason it is currently undergoing renovations and will be closed until 2013. However, there is small special exhibition which shows some of its most beautiful objects and tells the story of everyday life from over 3500 years ago. On display are Minoan house facades made from tiles, a board game, model ships, jewellery and a number of seals.

One of the most valuable pieces is a vessel in the shape of a bull's head carved from soapstone with rock crystal eyes and a mother of pearl mouth and a vessel made of shimmering rock crystal. The imaginative wall frescoes from the palace of Knossós and Minoan villas are also impressive.

Enquire about opening times at the museum | Platía Elef-therías/Odós Xanthudínu

ARSENAL

On the promenade close to the cruise ship terminal, are a number of Venetian arches from the 16th century which were used for storage and to repair ships during winter storms. *Freely accessible | at the fishing boat and yacht harbour*

BEMBO FOUNTAIN

Venetian fountain at the end of the market alley, built in 1588 using a Roman sarcophagus and statue. In front of the fountain are the chairs of a coffee house (*Budget*) that has its kitchen in an old Ottoman pump house. *Odós 1866*

HISTORICAL MUSEUM

The collection contains pieces from early Christian times up to the present. You can see costumes, maps, photos, coins, ceramics, jewellery and folk art; as well as the study of the poet Nikos Kazantzákis and even two small paintings by the famous painter El Greco. *Mon–Sat 9am–5pm, Wed until 9pm | entrance 5 euros | Odós Lip. Kalokerinú 7 | www.historical-museum.gr*

KÚLES FORTRESS ☼

The Venetian fortress (1523–40) offers a lovely view of the busy harbour. *Tue–Sun 8.30am–3pm | entrance 2 euros |at the breakwater of the fishing harbour*

LOGGIA

The meeting place of Venetian nobles has been restored and now serves as the town hall. *Interior viewing not allowed | Odós 25 Avgústu*

MOROSÍNI FOUNTAIN

This Iráklio landmark was built in 1628 by the Venetian governor Francesco Morosíni

to improve the water of the city. In front of the fountain are some glass slabs that protect the ruins of the medieval water pipes. *Platía Venizélou*

CITY WALL & KAZANTZÁKIS' TOMB ☼ ●

The city's 3½ km (2 mi) walls, fortified by seven bastions and four gates were built in the 16th century according to plans by the architect Michaele Sanmicheli. Nowadays they can only be entered at the Martinengo Bastion.

This is also where you will find the tomb of Crete's most famous poet Nikos Kazantzákis, creator of *Zorba the Greek*. Because of his unorthodox view of the world, city authorities did not allow him to be buried in the graveyard. His epitaph:

'I hope for nothing, I fear nothing, I am free' is on a simple wooden cross and is also often seen on T-shirts. *Admission free during the day | Martinengo Bastion (entrance from Odós Nikoláou Plastirá)*

FOOD & DRINK

INSIDERTIP KIRKOR AND PHYLLO...SOPHIES

Two cafés, rich in tradition, serve *bougátsa*, a type of semolina pudding with phyllo pastry, dusted with lots of icing sugar. A savoury version is the *bougátsa tirí* made with a sheeps' cheese filling. *Daily from 8am | Morosini Fountain | Budget*

INSIDERTIP PARASKEVÁS

Modern fish taverna in a small square behind the Historical Museum well away from the tourists. *Daily from 6pm | Pl. Kalokerinoú | Moderate–Expensive*

TOU TERZÁKI

An ouzeri where guests make their selection by ticking them off on a list. *Mon–Sat from 1pm | Odos Marinelli 17 | Moderate*

SHOPPING

The most interesting shopping street is the *Odós 1866,* a market street shaded by awnings. There are fruits, vegetables, meat, fish as well as herbs, *rakí* and cheeses and local specialities like Cretan wedding bread on offer. Fashion boutiques can be found in the *Odós Dédalu* and around the Morosíni Fountain and the most jewellery shops in the region of the Archaeological Museum while

Oriental feel: colourful awnings shade the market street Odós 1866

hemp products can be found at *Odós Korái*.

SPORTS & LEISURE

City buses make stops at the beaches close to the city. Surfboards can be rented and you can play tennis at the *Iráklio Tennis Club (Odos Dukos Beaufort | tel. 28 10 22 61 52)* or go bowling in at *Candia Bowling (Odos Therissos | tel. 28 10 25 66 52)*.

ENTERTAINMENT

In the evenings young people meet in the bars and music cafés at ● *Platía Korái* while a more alternative public frequent the little bars in the *Odós Chandakós*. Dance clubs open around midnight in *Odós Epimenídu* and at the western edge of the old town at *S. Venizélu*

INSIDER TIP TERIRÉM

Meeting place for the locals with live Cretan music but it only opens sporadically during peak season as the musicians are travelling through Crete performing at village festivals. *Autumn–early summer Fri/Sat from 11pm | Odós Andréa Papandréou 255 | Ammoudára*

VENÉTO ⛄ ●

Romantic bar with views of the harbour in an old Venetian house in the old town is perfect for a quiet evening out. They offer different kinds of coffees and colourful cocktails. Popular with couples and young women. *Odos Epimenidu 7–9*

WHERE TO STAY

IRÍNI

This modern eight-storey hotel is very central and offers the best value for money in town. The private car park has place for 40 cars. *59 rooms | Odós Idomenéos 4 | tel. 28 10 22 97 03 | www.irini-hotel.gr | Budget*

LENA

Affordable old town hotel, peaceful and centrally situated. Cosy atmosphere and simple furnishings. Some of the rooms only have a single bath per floor. *16 rooms | Odós Lachaná 10 | tel. 28 10 22 32 80 | www.lena-hotel.gr | Budget–Moderate*

MÉGARON

A luxury hotel that opened in 2003, it is in a prestigious 1930s building with an indoor and outdoor pool. *58 rooms | Odós Dúkos Beaufort 9 | tel. 28 10 30 53 00 | www.gdmmegaron.gr | Expensive*

INSIDER TIP SOFIA

Comfortable family-run hotel with small pool and private parking situated 1½ mi from the airport and 250 m from a bus stop. It is ideal for tourists with cars who want to avoid driving in the city, as well as for an overnight stay at the start or end of the holiday. *69 rooms | Odós Stadíou 57 | Néa Alikarnássos | tel. 28 10 24 00 02 | www.hotel-sofia.gr | Moderate*

INFORMATION

GREEK NATIONAL TOURISM ORGANISATION

Tel. 28 10 22 82 03 | Odós Xanthulídu (across the Archaeological Museum)

WHERE TO GO

ANÓGIA
(138 C2) (*⑭ J4*)

German troops destroyed this village in 1944 – as revenge for the villagers' possible involvement in the abduction of General von Kreipe to Egypt – and shot all the male inhabitants. A memorial plaque in the large modern town hall commemorates the event. There are still a few old houses and pretty squares in the lower part of the village where signposts show the way to the *Alkiwíades Skulás Grílios Museum*. The woodcarver and naive painter always depicted the Cretan fight for independence. At *Kafenío Grílios* you can ask for the custodian who will not only unlock the museum for you but also serenade you with his *lýra*. *43 km (26 mi)*

ARCHÁNES
(140 A3) (*W L4*)

This large winegrowers' village with 3500 inhabitants at the foot of the imposing *Júchtas* (811 m), has been settled since the Minoan times. On Fúrni hill at the village entrance is a *Minoan necropolis (Tue–Sun 8.30am–2.30pm | admission free)*. 5 km (3 mi) from the village on the northern face of Júchtas are the remains

of a *Minoan temple (only visible from outside)*, where people were sacrificed in the 17th century BC – possibly to placate the gods and to prevent the earthquakes which destroyed the palaces and the temples itself. A small *museum in the main road recounts its history (Wed–Mon 8.30am–3pm | admission free)*. *16 km (10 mi)*

CHERSÓNISOS
(140 B–C2) (*W M3*)

This is one of the largest tourism centres on Crete. It consists of an old village with a beautiful square and green surroundings and the resort area of *Liménas Chersónisou* with hotels, dance clubs and tavernas. The sand and pebble beaches are too small for the large number of tourists who visit.

The remains of two early Christian churches with floor mosaics lie in the west of the village centre on a small peninsula above the harbour and to the east of the village in the grounds of the Eri Beach hotel. On the beach promenade is a ● *Roman fountain* that dates from the 3rd century, with fish and other marine mosaics. The private *open air museum Lychnostátis (Sun–Fri 9am–2pm | entrance 5 euros)* is worth a visit. Only about 20 minutes by foot from the hustle and bustle of Chersónisos are the two villages of *Kutulufári* and *Piskopianó* on a mountain slope. Their narrow alleyways and stone houses make them quite idyllic. *26 km (16 mi)*

FÓDELE
(139 D1) (*W J3*)

In this village in between orange and olive groves the painter Doménikos Theotokópulos was born in 1541. He later became known worldwide as El Greco. The home in which he was born *(May–Sept daily 9am–7pm, April–Nov daily 8.30am–3pm | admission free)* has been wonderfully reconstructed. A lovely *kafenío* and a church from the 10th century are in front of it. The church has a mosaic depicting fishermen at work. *29 km (18 mi)*

GOÚRNES
(140 B2) (*ⓜ L3*)

Above the resort swimming area is an old American communications base, a large part of the area is a desolate track of abandoned barracks.

In 2005 it became home to the largest and most modern aquarium in southern Europe, the ● *CretAquarium* with more than 2500 creatures from 200 different species. It has webcams, computer screens and a cinema, all using state-of-the-art technology. *Well signposted | May–Sept daily 9.30am–9pm, Oct–April daily 9.30am–5pm | entrance 8 euros, children (5–17 years), seniors from 65 years and students 6 euros | www.cretaquarium.gr. 16 km (10 mi)*

KERÁ
(140 C3) (*ⓜ M4*)

Just below the 560 m (1836 ft) high mountain village on the road from Chersónisos to the Lassíthi Plateau, the *Panagía i Kerá Monastery (daily 8am–1pm and 4–7pm | entrance 3 euros)* emerges from the lush greenery that surrounds it. Its 14th century church is filled with beautiful frescoes. *46 km (28 mi)*

KNOSSÓS ★ (139 F2) (*ⓜ L4*)
MAP ON PAGE 66

The Minoan palace of Knossós has to be the starting point for anyone interested in Cretan archaeology. The reconstruction that was started in 1900 by Sir Arthur Evans took 40 years to finish and holds the key to a better understanding of the other Minoan palaces and villas. The complex was the centre of government, administration and culture in Crete from 2000 to 1450 BC. It consisted of about

The artist El Greco's bust in Fódele, his birthplace

1400 rooms (some of them up to 4 floors high). The centre of the palace was a 53 m (173 ft) long 28 m (91 ft) wide centre courtyard which may have been used for games, cultural events and processions.

From the western court of the palace, a winding processional corridor leads to the centre courtyard. In the west side, Evans excavated several interesting rooms. The pillar crypt is interpreted as a chapel and the rooms leading off it are said to be treasure chambers.

One of the rooms has an alabaster throne that stands opposite a water basin. Stone benches are situated along the walls. This throne room was reached via a lobby lined with more wall benches and a copy of a wooden throne. Evans believed that this was a waiting room where the Minoans waited to have an audience with Minos. The ruler sat on his throne and kept snakes in the basin as a symbol of his power. Evans may have been wrong and the throne could have been kept empty for a deity as was the case in Egypt with the Throne of Isis. When visiting Knossós you should keep in mind there is no written record about the Minoan era and that conclusions drawn from the excavations are mostly speculative. It may be that Evans was influenced by Buckingham Palace

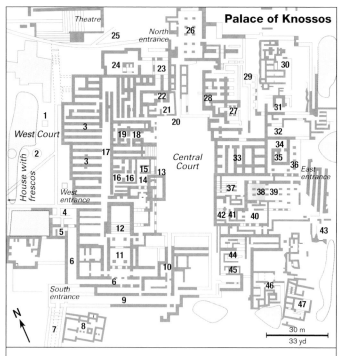

Palace of Knossos

1 Altar base	17 Storeroom corridor	33 Room with water basin
2 Circular pits	18 Throne room	34 Potter's workshops
3 Storerooms	19 Cult chamber	35 Stone mason's workshop
4 West Propylaea	20 North ramp	36 East veranda
5 Guard room	21 Prison	37 Staircase
6 Processional corridor	22 Cult chamber	38 Hall of Double Axes
7 Columned staircase	23 North-west Propylaea	39 King's Megaron
8 South house	24 Cult area	40 Queen's Megaron
9 South corridor	25 Royal Road	41 Queen's bathroom
10 Corridor	26 Custom house	42 Queen's dressing room
11 South Propylaea	27 North-east Hall	43 Eastern bastion
12 Staircase	28 North-east storerooms	44 Shrine of Double Axes
13 Shrine	29 Potter's workshops (?)	45 Lustral basin
14 Antechamber	30 Potter's workshops	46 House of the Chancel Screen
15 Central shrine	31 Storeroom	47 South-east house
16 Pillar crypt	32 Light well	

when it came to interpreting some of the rooms as the private quarters of the king and queen as well as changing rooms, bathrooms and sleeping quarters. In some of the storage chambers, man-sized vessels were found which are believed to have contained oil, wine and grain. Also identifiable are the workshops of a potter and a stone mason as well as tower like structures at the edge of the palace which could have been used as watchtowers and customs offices. In the north-western part of the palace is an area with terraced steps with seating for 500 people but the reason why people may have gathered there has not been established.

Around 3500 years ago Knossós would have had about 10,000 inhabitants and its harbour was Amnissós. When the Minoan empire fell in 1450 BC, the ruins remained occupied for quite some time. They must have been just as impressive to the Achaear and Dorians as they are for us today. This may be how the myth of the Minotaur developed, the winding and twisting hallways of the palace being interpreted as a labyrinth.

Today's visitors can have a clearer idea of the labyrinth: everywhere in the souvenir shops are imaginative drawings that attempt to reconstruct how the palace may once have looked. *Daily 8.30am–7.30pm (in winter 8.30am–5pm) | entrance 6 euros, combi-ticket with Archaeological Museum (if open) 10 euros. From Iráklio the city bus no. 2 leaves from the bus station at the harbour and from the bus stop in front of house number 62 in Odos 1821, every 20 minutes to Knossós, which is only 5 km (3 mi).*

Start with the palace of Knossós if you want to understand Minoan culture

The colourful frescoes in Knossós are almost 3500 years old

MÁLIA
(140 C2) (*M–N4*)

This resort on the northern coast has lovely sandy beaches and water sport possibilities and its historical village centre south of the coast road still has some Cretan charm. The best taverna in the village centre is **INSIDER TIP** *Kalesma* (daily from 6pm | Odós Omirú | reservations recommended | tel. 28 97 03 31 25 | *Expensive*). Small, typically Cretan dishes are served.

Between the coastal road and the sea, east of the village are the ruins of the Minoan *palace of Mália*, with the same structure as Knossós – storage rooms, west and central courtyards, processional routes, an amphitheatre and chapels. Guided tours are also presented in English (*Tue–Sun 8.30am–3pm | entrance 4 euros, guided tour 4 euros*). *37 km (23 mi)*

MIRTIÁ
(139 F3) (*L4*)

Wine growers' village that is home to the *Kazantzákis Museum* (May–Oct daily 9am–5pm, Nov–April, Sun 10am–3pm | *entrance 3 euros*) where memorabilia from Crete's greatest poet and playwright are on display along with some of the original costumes from theatre productions. *25 km (15 mi)*

NÍDA PLATEAU ★ ●
(138 C3) (*J4*)

This almost 1400 m (4600 ft) high plateau belongs to the village *Anógia*. It can be reached via the 21 km (13 mi) road and serves as a grazing area for sheep and goats. The proprietor of the state-owned taverna (which also has a few beds for visitors) will show hiking enthusiasts the way to the famous (but closed for visitors) 1540 m (5052 ft) high Ída cave. A large number of offerings in the form of gold and silver jewellery, spearheads and seals from Minoan to Roman times have been found in the cave. This cave, just like the Psichró cave on the Lassíthi Plateau, is said to be the birthplace of Zeus. *65 km (40 mi)*

TÍLISSOS
(139 D2) (*K4*)

The remains of three Minoan homes can be seen in an idyllic setting at the edge of the town. They had two floors; the ground floor had storage rooms, workshops and labourers' rooms while the upper floor housed the owners in 3 to 4 roomed apartments. (*Tue–Sun 8.30am–3pm | entrance 2 euros*). *15 km (9¼ mi)*

ZONIANÁ
(138 C2) (*J4*)

At the edge of this mountain village lies the 550 m (1800 ft) ● *Sventóni stalactite cave*, which can be viewed with a guide (daily 9am–6pm, Nov–March only Fri–Sun

9.30am–4pm | entrance 4 euros | www.zoniana.gr). In the *waxworks museum Potamiós* important milestones in the Cretan history have been recreated *(daily 10am–2.30pm and 5–9pm | entrance 4 euros)*. 43 km (26 mi)

MÁTALA

(138 B5) (*ᗰ H6*) **During the 1960s this isolated fishermen's village became well known as a hippie paradise.**

Today it has grown considerably and now stretches 2000 m into the interior. The wide sandy beaches have remained as have the caves where the hippies used to live but the former fishermen's houses have been converted into tavernas. Tourists mainly stay in small guest houses close to the beach while package tours prefer the new hotels further inland. Many day visitors also arrive daily making Mátala a significant south coast resort but one that still manages to retain its relaxed ambiance.

SIGHTSEEING

CAVES
The easily accessible caves in the cliffs were ideal for hippies as the Romans had carved out tombs and tables for their funeral banquets which made the caves quite comfortable.

ROMAN SETTLEMENT
On the right hand side of the road towards Red Beach are the remains of a Roman harbour settlement, which is open for viewing.

FOOD & DRINK

AKUNA MATATA
Restaurant and bar in the fishermen's quarter with hammocks on the roof garden and live music (from *lýra* to rock) on certain evenings in summer. Good menu selection and large portions. *Daily from 9am | Moderate*

SHOPPING

AXEL GENTHNER
German goldsmith Making unique gold and silver creations. *Daily 6–8.30pm | in the shopping area at the Hotel Zafiria*

SPORTS & LEISURE

MÁTALA BEACH
This beach with its coarse sand and crystal blue water is 200 m (656 ft) long and 40 m (131 ft) wide. The southern half is lined with tavernas and on the northern side, behind trees, there is a camping site. No water sport activities.

RED BEACH
Mátala has a road that is lined with guest houses which has a pathway that leads to Red Beach with its red shimmering sand. The walk takes approx. 30 minutes, umbrellas can be hired and nudity is the norm.

ENTERTAINMENT

CALDERA
Small lounge bar on the outer seaside edge of the fishermen's quarter, gives you the feeling of being on a boat. Those who come here prefer to sit in silence or to chat with friends and not to dance.

WHERE TO STAY

MÁTALA VIEW
17 studios, apartments and rooms close the beach and village centre. *Tel. 28 92 04 5114 | www.matala-apartments.com | Budget*

MÁTALA

WHERE TO GO

AGÍA TRIÁDA
(138 C5) (ΩΩ H5)

In the west of the Messará Plateau a three-winged estate was built close to the Minoan palace of Festós in 1600 BC. Today only the foundation walls remain. *Daily 8.30am–3pm | entrance 3 euros, with Festós 6 euros. 10 km (6 mi)*

FESTÓS ★ ≈
(138 C5) (ΩΩ J5)

In Minoan times the centre of the fertile Messará Plateau was the palace of Festós, laid out in a series of low ridge terraces. All that is left of the original central court-yard (which has a similar layout to Knossós) are the remains of the north and west wing. The other two were destroyed by an earthquake in 1450 BC. A striking feature is the 13.75 m (45 ft) wide and 20 m (65 ft) long stairway which dates back to the original palace construction. Guests seated on the terraced steps could watch cult rituals being performed as if in a theatre. As at Knossós, the storage rooms, ceremonial basins for ritual washing and large rooms (possibly the living quarters of the ruling family) are all identifiable *(daily 8am–7pm, Nov–May until 5pm | entrance 4 euros, with Agía Triáda 6 euros). 10 km (6 mi)*

GÓRTIS
(139 D5) (ΩΩ J5)

On either side of the main road between Iráklio and Festós lie remains of the island's

The hippie caves are empty, but the area around Mátala and its beaches is still popular

Roman capital. At the northern entrance, you will find the remains of the *Títus Basilica* from the 6th century. Saint *Títus*, the first bishop of the island, never actually held mass here, but his skull was kept as a relic here until 1669.

From the ancient *agorá* you can go to the Roman *odéon,* a theatre for music and poetry performances. Covered with a roof and behind iron bars, are twelve (there were 20) law tablets which date back to about 500 BC. The civic and penal law of the Doric city of Górtis are inscribed on 42 stone blocks with 17,000 letters (in lines written from left to right and right to left) and are a unique testimony to ancient law *(daily 9am–7.30pm, Nov– May until 3pm | entrance 4 euros)*. Guided tours are limited to the most important

ruins north of the road but it is worth walking through the olive groves on the south side of the road where ● relics of the city (that gave sanctuary to Hannibal) can also be seen. *19 km (11¾ mi)*

MÍRES
(138 C5) (*ω J5*)

Every Saturday afternoon, this little village in the fertile Messará Plateau showcases INSIDERTIP one of Crete's largest weekly markets. On sale are not only fruit and veggies, but also textiles, tools and household products. *13 km (8 mi)*

PITSÍDIA
(138 C5) (*ω H6*)

This attractive village is a good alternative to Mátala. The platía is the main meeting place. At *Ouzerí Fábrika* locals and guests sometimes get together to play music. For a swim you can go to *Kómo beach* 2500 m away, where you can see the fenced off excavations of a Minoan harbour settlement. *4 km (2.4 mi)*

VÓRI ★
(138 C5) (*ω J5*)

The peaceful village on the edge of the Messará Plateau has an attractive and interesting *Folk Museum (April–Oct daily 10am–6pm | entrance 3 euros)*. Exhibits from everyday life from the last three to five centuries are well presented and explained. *14 km (8¾ mi)*

ZARÓS ★
(139 D4) (*ω J5*)

This large town on the 340 m (1115 ft) high southern slope of the Ída Mountain is well known for its trout farming and its many beautiful hiking possibilities. INSIDERTIP Two good *trout tavernas (Moderate)* are situated on the road to the little mountain lake of Záros. *25 km (15 mi)*

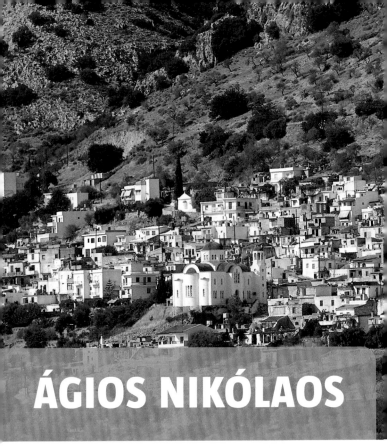

ÁGIOS NIKÓLAOS

The Venetians saw the beautiful wide bay and peaceful countryside named it Mirabéllo, Italian for 'lovely view'. Here the majestic Cretan mountains seem to be holding back, leaving just enough space on the western and southern shores for the small provincial capital of eastern Crete, named after Saint Nicholas and for Eloúnda, the Cretan village with the most luxury resorts.

The coast is very well laid out and structured in such a way that the hotels don't look out of place or overdeveloped. The everyday lives of the locals and the tourists also seem to mix together quite harmoniously.

Peaceful old villages slumber on the peninsula in the north-west, with the wide bay stretching out before them. The fertile plains of the Lassíthi Plateau, which are covered with snow until early in spring, are used intensively for agricultural purposes, but do take a few days of your holiday and spend it in the countryside amongst the locals there.

In this small area there are numerous examples of all the various eras in Crete's long cultural history and if the Gulf of Mirabéllo is your holiday destination, you will not need to travel too far to have a very fulfilling holiday.

Photo: The mountain village of Krítsa

Sleepy villages: the hinterland beyond the Mirabéllo Gulf region has retained its unspoilt rural Cretan character

ÁGIOS NIKÓLAOS

MAP INSIDE BACK COVER
(141 E3–4) (*m̨* *O4*) **The small town (pop. 10,000) can accommodate 20,000 guests during the summer and even during the peak season, it retains its charm.**

There are cafés on the shore of the inland lake but tourists are also drawn to the many cafés along the long coast of the peninsula, the harbour and yacht marina as well as the shops in the pedestrian zone. Ágios, as the locals call it, has developed organically and without plans. The town is at its most beautiful on the shore of the small lake *Límni Vulisméni*, which was connected with the harbour by a 61 m (200 ft) long and 12 m (40 ft) wide channel in 1870. It is surrounded by tales and legends. Fifty years ago, after the eruption of the Santorini volcano, the lake water rose up and dead fish washed ashore. Since then, many Cretans believe that there is an underground connection between the lake and the ocean.

Odós 28 Octowríu making up the city centre. The yacht marina is also in the south. There is a small sand and pebble beach on the peninsula with another one at the south-western end of the marina. Not many people swim in the sea in Ágios, they prefer the hotel pools, or take taxis, boats or buses to beaches in the vicinity.

Taverna paradise on lake Límni Vulisméni, which is connected with the sea by a small channel

Fishing boats line both sides of the lake, which is surrounded by rocky cliffs. Here you will also find tables and chairs set out by café owners. The views from these cliff top cafés are just breathtaking, overlooking the lake and the harbour.

Running between the harbour and another bay on the peninsula's southern section are the main business streets Odós El. Venizélou, Odós Kundurá and

SIGHTSEEING

AGÍA TRIÁDA CHURCH

The modern main church, at Platía El. Venizélos, has been decorated with frescoes in the traditional Byzantine style. Although they lack the charm that comes with age, they are worth a visit because of the fresh colours and good light. *Mostly 7am–noon and 4–7.30pm | admission free*

ÁGIOS NIKÓLAOS CHURCH

This little church must be very old. Inside one can just make out traces of frescoes with symbols instead of those of Christ and the saints. This means that it must date back to the 8th or 9th century. Only for those who have a particular interest. *Located in the grounds of the Minos Palace Hotel and the key is available (with a deposit) at the reception desk.*

ARCHAEOLOGICAL MUSEUM

A museum that is well worth a visit, it has numerous exhibits from eastern Crete including some interesting idols and beautiful vases as well as the Goddess of Mírtos, an early Minoan vessel decorated with the characteristics of a female figure with a phallus shaped neck and arms extended to hold a type of container. Another exceptional item is a skull dating back to the 1st century. It is decorated with a gold wreath and has a coin in its mouth, the coin is believed to have been payment for the ferry to the underworld. *Tue–Sun 8.30am–3pm | entrance 3 euros | Odós Paleológu 68*

FOLK MUSEUM

A small, well organised museum on the canal bridge showing traditional woven and embroidered pieces, wood carvings and costumes. Also interesting are the photos from the 1930s, when foreigners were still a rarity in Ágios. *Sun–Fri 10am–4pm | entrance 3 euros | next to the taxi stands on the bridge*

IRIS MUSEUM

A museum housed in a villa that dates back to 1899. It showcases Crete's flora by using photos and dried herbs and plants. The exhibits all have good English explanation. *Fri–Wed 9am–1pm and 5.30–8.30pm | entrance 2 euros | Odós 28is Octovríou 21*

MUNICIPAL GALLERY

Temporary exhibitions of modern art, photography and design. *Mid June–Oct daily 11am–2pm, 6.30–9pm | admission free | Odós 28is Octovríou 8*

FOOD & DRINK

DE MOLEN

A Dutch restaurant situated above the sea. Pancake dishes until 6pm. *Mon–Sat from 10am, Sun from noon | Odós D. Solomú | Moderate*

ÍTANOS

A modern taverna with a wide selection of dishes. Recommended for lunch and not a romantic dinner. Take a look at the food trays first, they are more informative than the menu. *Daily 10am–11pm | Odós Kípru 1 | Moderate*

MARCO POLO HIGHLIGHTS

★ **Goúrnia**
See how the Minoans lived: the ruins of a 3500-year old city → p. 79

★ **Krítsa**
This mountain village is picture-perfect and also has some of the island's most beautiful Byzantine frescoes → p. 80

★ **Lassíthi Plateau**
A fertile mountain oasis with ancient caves, beautiful villages and a folk museum → p. 80

★ **Spinalónga**
A lepers' village built within the walls of a Venetian fortress → p. 83

MIGÓMIS ☄

This gourmet restaurant on the high cliffs of the Vulisméni lake offer views of the lake and harbour and the Gulf of Mirabéllo. In the evenings, this view is very romantic, with a pianist entertaining guests. The kitchen offers Mediterranean food like risotto with wild mushrooms, swordfish carpaccio or lamb cutlets with mint sauce. Comprehensive wine list. *Daily from noon | Odós N. Plastíra 20 | Expensive*

PÉLAGOS

A taverna situated in a classically Greek house. The *kaiki* boat at the entrance is a symbol of their speciality: fish and seafood. Shady garden full of flowers. Plenty of good wines. *Daily noon–midnight | Odós Str. Koráka 10 | Expensive*

SHOPPING

CHEZ SONJA

A wide variety of good quality traditional Cretan woven articles, jewellery and ceramics. *Odós 28is Octovríu 20*

KERÁ

Lovely shop with tasteful items (both new and old); woven articles, jewellery, marionettes and dolls from Greek workshops. *Odós J. Kundurú 8 (at the harbour underneath the restaurant Cretan Stars)*

FRESH MARKET

A large weekly market takes place every Wednesday morning on *Odós Ethnikís Antistáseo.*

SPORTS & BEACHES

You can play tennis and basketball in the stadium Aktí Atlantídos and various water sports are offered by the big hotels on the way to Eloúnda. You can also go horseback riding in the nearby town of Exo Lakónia *(tel. 28 41 02 42 46 and 28 41 02 69 43).*

The most beautiful beach is the almost 120 m long pebble beach *Kitroplatía beach*, about 3 minutes from the harbour. Along the coastal road to Eloúnda, at the edge of town, lies the sandy *Havanía*

CRETAN MULTITASKER

On the road from Ágios Nikólaos to the Lassíthi Plateau, Manólis Farsáris has established a tourist supermarket in the nearly uninhabited village of Zénia. Every year he builds another room by himself. There is even a bar and café where he serves *rakómeli (rakí* mixed with honey) as well as ice-cream, snacks and fresh juice. In the shop section he sells anything from Korean jeans to cheap icons, spoons that are carved by his grandfather and gods made from plaster of Paris. But he also offers his guests another little service: on the

pavement outside he has set up a pair of binoculars on an old umbrella stand with a picture that he drew himself in which he details everything that you can see through the binoculars. Next to it he has some slingshots hanging from a branch of a tree for children to play with. A few feet away a multilingual handwritten sign tells you that the tables and chairs on the terrace can be used at no cost for picnics if you bring your own picnic baskets. Manólis has to feed his family and he is attempting to do so in his own unique Cretan way!

Kitroplatía beach in Agios is seldom overcrowded

beach. Almost 1500 m south-east of the town, you will find the 250 m long sandy *Almirós beach*, some 1500 m further along the road to Sitía lies the sandy 100 m long *Ammoudará beach*. Tavernas, deck-chairs and umbrellas are everywhere.

ENTERTAINMENT

There are plenty of clubs and nightclubs here and they are concentrated around the harbour and the eastern edge of the town. Last meeting place for night owls is the café at the ferry pier.

ALÉXANDROS
Music bar in a roof garden with a view of the sea, decorated with flowers. Dance music for every age and taste. The DJ even plays oldies on request. *Daily from 8pm | Odós Kondiláki 1*

ARMÍDA
A replica of an old sailing ship in the inner harbour is a popular meeting place – enjoy cocktails as you are rocked by the gentle waves of the sea. *Daily from noon | in the harbour in front of Aktí J. Koundoúrou*

INSIDER TIP PERÍPOU
This café high above the sea also sells CDs and books as well as being an internet café. Locals and tourists mingle from 10pm with wine, frappés and cocktails. *Daily from 10pm | Odós 28is Octovríou 25*

CORAL

The hotel consists of two terraced buildings interlinked by a pool terrace. There is no beach on the opposite side of the coastal road but you can access the water for a swim. Good place to overnight. *172 rooms | Aktí Iosíf Koundoúrou | tel. 28 41 02 83 63 | www.mhotels.gr | Moderate–Expensive*

DU LAC

One of the few hotels that are situated directly on the lake's shore. A room with a view of the lake makes up for the fact that vehicles cannot park close to the hotel. *24 rooms | Odós 28is Octovríou | tel. 28 41 02 27 11 | www.dulachotel.gr | Budget*

MINOS PALACE ☆

Large hotel with 288 beds. Located 800 m from the town on a peninsula. Large swimming pool, two tennis courts and a dive school. Taxi boats into the town centre. *Aktí Ilía Sotirú | tel. 28 41 02 38 01 | www.mamidakishotels.gr | Expensive*

INSIDER TIP PALAZZO

A four storey house with ten tastefully decorated two-bedroom apartments, it is located at the edge of the central part of town, at the Kitroplatía beach. Bathrooms and kitchenettes are well stocked, ☆ eight of the apartments have sea views. On the ground level there is a café as well as a good restaurant, *Bárko* (*Moderate*). Here you will be both in the centre and near the beach and well looked after by the Dermitzákis family. *Odós Tselépi 18/Aktí Pagkálou | tel. 28 41 02 50 80 | Moderate*

INSIDER TIP PÉRGOLA

This hotel is a family business run by Jánnis und Stélla. It is situated on the tip

Eloúnda's fishermen supply the restaurants and hotels in the region with seafood

of the peninsula close to the ferry pier. Rooms on the top floor have sea views. *26 rooms | Odós Sarolídi 20 | tel. 28 41 02 8152 | Budget*

MUNICIPAL TOURIST INFORMATION OFFICE
On the bridge between the sea and the harbour | tel. 28 41 02 23 57 | www.aghios nikolaos.eu

WHERE TO GO

ELOÚNDA
(141 E3) (*ⓜ O4*)
The coast around Eloúnda has the most exclusive luxury hotels on the island. Greek politicians, international film and pop stars love to holiday here. Those not staying here can only gain entrance by reserving a table at one of the gourmet restaurants or by going for a treatment in one of the spas. The best spa on the island, belongs to the ● *Blue Palace Resort (tel. 28 41 06 55 00 | www.bluepalace.gr | Expensive)*. The spa is also open to non-residents and the thalassic therapy is especially recommended.
Eloúnda is connected with the island of *Spinalónga* by a causeway. The ancient city of *Olús* was situated here, but today the only traces of the city remain underwater, like the early Christian floor mosaic close to the taverna at the dam.
Many of Eloúnda's restaurants are along the coast in the direction of Olús but the best food is in the taverna *Mariléna* on the coast road. The proprietors Michális and Dímitris are originally from Cyprus and serve an INSIDER TIP excellent *mesé*, a dish made up of small portions of many different dishes. Once weekly a Cretan evening is held *(daily from noon | Moderate)*. *12 km (7 mi)*

FANEROMÉNIS MONASTERY
(141 F4) (*ⓜ O5*)
The monastery (which is occupied during summer) sits high above the Gulf of Mirabéllo and can only be reached via a winding road, where the sheep and goats far outnumber the vehicles. The monastery's centre is a cave converted into a church – legend has it that a shepherd found an icon of Mary during the Byzantine era – and it still attracts many pilgrims on the 14th and 15th of August. The monks are very friendly, although not always in residence as they have to assist villages without priests during certain times. When the monks are absent, the monastery is closed. *(When open, daily 7am– noon and 5–7pm). 23 km (14 mi)*

GOÚRNIA ★ ☆
(141 F4) (*ⓜ O–P5*)
On the coastal road on a low hill above the Gulf of Mirabéllo are the excavations of the Minoan city Goúrnia. The foundation walls of the 3 500 year old houses are in good condition and parts of the stairways that led to the upper floor can still be seen. Narrow, paved alleys lead to the palace higher up on the hill. *Tue–Sun 8.30am–3 pm | entrance 2 euros | 19 km (11¾ mi)*

KÁSTELLI (141 E3) (*ⓜ O4*)
With its old Venetian mansions and artfully wrought gates and railings, this village is one of the most beautiful in the region. Its narrow streets are full of wild geraniums. An alley lined with eucalyptus trees leads you into the neighbouring village of *Fourní,* where almond trees blossom at the end of March. Here, at the village square María Sfiráki awaits you in her taverna *Plátanos* underneath an old tree where she serves fresh salads and affordable dishes like rabbit or lamb's liver *(daily from 9am | Budget)*.

A track leads to the excavations of the Dorian city *Dríros,* where the remains of an Apollo temple, cistern, altar and the Agorá can still be seen. *Admission free| 20 km (13 mi)*

KATHARÓ PLATEAU
(141 D4) *(∅ N5)*

From *Krítsa* a 17 km (11 mi) long road leads up to the 1150 m (3780 ft) high lonely plateau. The plateau is used to farm fruit, grapes and grains. People only live here between 20 May and 30 November, and during this time the *kafenía* and tavernas are also open. An important festival of the Virgin Mary is celebrated on the 6th of August. *28 km (17 mi)*

to 17th century. The dome in the nave does not show Christ as the ruler of all, instead there are four scenes from the New Testament: Mary in the temple, the baptism of Jesus, the resurrection of Lazarus and Jesus' entrance into Jerusalem on Palm Sunday. In the centre of the dome, four angels represent heaven. The prophets of the Old Testament that prophesised the coming of Christ are depicted on the lower edge. In the nave the testimonies of Matthew, Mark, Luke and John can be seen. Even for those not interested in theology, the images of hell on the west wall will leave a strong impression. *(April–Oct only Tue–Sun 8.30am–3pm | entrance 3 euros). 9 km (5½ mi)*

Panagía i Kerá: well preserved frescoes offer a remarkable view of heaven and hell

KRÍTSA ★ (141 E4) *(∅ O5)*

This pretty and very popular mountain village has plenty of souvenir shops, cafés and tavernas as well as a Byzantine art jewel: the *Panagía i Kerá* church with perfectly intact frescoes dating from the 15th

LASSÍTHI PLATEAU ★
(140–141 C–D–E 3–4) *(∅ M–N 4–5)*

Crete's most fertile plateau lies at an altitude of 800 m (2624 ft) in the Díkti mountain range. It is almost 10 km (6 mi) long and 5 km (3 mi) wide. The groundwater which lies just beneath its surface was pumped into the fields by sailed windmills up until the 1970s. Tour operators still use the image of these windmills in advertising even though there are hardly left as they have been replaced by motorised pumps. If you travel on your own it is best to do a round trip: drive to *Stalída* (134 C2) *(ꟿ M4)* on the northern coast, then via *Mochós* and the 900 m (3000 ft) high *Àmbelos Afín* pass (134 C3) *(ꟿ M4)* on to the plain which you then travel around in an anti-clockwise direction. Leave at *Mésa Lasíthi* (141 D4) *(ꟿ N4)* and return via *Zénia* (141 D3) *(ꟿ N4)* and *Neápoli* (141 D3) *(ꟿ N4)* back to the coastal motorway.

The main attraction on the plateau is the *stalactite cave Diktéon Ándron (daily 9am–3pm, May–Sept until 7pm / entrance 4 euros)* above the village of *Psychró* (140 C4) *(ꟿ N5)*. This was a place of worship from as early as the 2nd century BC. According to legend, it was here that Zeus was brought up by goats because his mother Rhea feared that his father Kronos would see him as a rival and devour him as he had Zeus' siblings. It is possible to ride up to the cave on donkeys. The cave is well lit and sturdy footwear is recommended.

It is worth spending at least one night on the plateau. Recommended is the *Pension Maria (16 rooms / enquire at the Hotel Rea in the centre/ tel. 28 44 03 17 74 | Budget)* in the large village *Ágios Geórgios* where there is also an interesting folk museum with an adjacent gallery *(daily 10am–4pm/entrance 2 euros)*. The ☺ **INSIDER TIP** *holiday homes Villaéti* in the neighbouring village Ágios Konstantínos *(5 houses / tel. 28 44 03 19 83 | www.vilaeti.gr | Expensive)* have a museum-like feel. A local family has lovingly restored the old village houses and decorated them with traditional details. Those who stay here sleep

An arduous climb to Zeus' 'nursery' Diktéon Ándron

in an environment that harks back to a bygone era and can also enjoy various Lassíthian specialities at the ☺ *Taverna Villaéti* which belongs to the same family and is situated in the main road. The sister of the proprietor is one of the pioneers of the organic potato cultivation on the plateau. *45 km (28 mi)*

LATÓ ✂
(141 E4) *(ꟿ O4)*

On a mountain north of Krítsa, with a view of Ágios Nikólaos, archaeologist have excavated the impressive remains of a Dorian city from the 7th to the 4th century BC: a small theatre, a cistern, the Agorá, foundations of a temple, a portico, a number of homes and the ruins of the city wall *(April–Oct, Tue–Sun 8.30am–3pm | entrance 2 euros)*. *3 km (1¾ mi)*

MÍLATOS (141 D2) (*ω N3*)

Mílatos is a small, unspoiled village at the edge of a coastal plain surrounded by mountains. A narrow road connects it coastal settlement *Paralía Milátu,* which is becoming more and more popular with tourists.

It is worth making the 4 km (2½ mi) detour from the village to the well signposted 🔆 *stalactite cave Milátu (admission free, torches recommended)*. A 45 m stretch has eight entrances and the main entrance leads directly to the largest cave, from where, after a short climb, you can reach the chapel of the apostle Thomas which was consecrated in 1935. It was built in memory of 3600 Cretans that were killed here, or taken into captivity to be sold as slaves in 1823 by the Ottomans.

LOW BUDGET

30 animal species live in the back of the cave, amongst them three kinds of bats, which with some luck, you may see at sunset. The view from the cave is worth the ten minute walk at any time of the day. *22 km (13.6)*

PLÁKA (141 E2) (*ω O3*)

This former fishing village is a booming holiday destination with all the associated overdevelopment. However, it is also an excellent surfing spot with a surf school and there are also excursion boats that go out the lepers' island *Kalidón*. Two excellent fish tavernas are *Maria's* and *Spinalónga* in the main road as well as *George* right on the beach *(all Moderate)*. *18 km (11 mi)*

PRÍNA (141 E5) (*ω O5*)

Small undiscovered village south of Ágios Nikólaos worth a visit in the late afternoon. The 🙂 taverna *Pitópoulis (Budget)* has a romantic setting with tables under some olive trees and **INSIDER TIP** proprietor Dímitris is a well known *lýra* player. He plays one evening a week for locals and guests *(mostly Wed | tel. 69 73 46 60 21)*. For MARCO POLO readers though he will sometimes even play his *lýra* during the day, if he has some time to spare. In the kitchen, Dímitris and his wife María only use olive oil from their own olives and the fish and vegetables are sourced locally. *19 km (11¾ mi)*

SÍSI (141 D2) (*ω N3*)

Once a fishing village, now a lovely little holiday village. It lies on a 150 m long, narrow fjord-like bay which is part of its appeal. At the entrance of the bay is a tiny beach and on the other side are the tables of tavernas and cafés on the beach promenade. There are three good sand and pebble beaches situated about 1500 m east of the village centre.

The hotel *Porto Sísi (15 rooms | tel. 28 41 07 13 85 | www.portosisi.com | Moderate)* is situated close to the village centre and directly on the coast and is a good accommodation option. If you prefer hotels that

selves inside a well preserved Venetian fortress. Amongst the lepers were craftsmen and farmers, a hairdresser and even a priest; people married and had children. Healthy newborn babies were im-

On Spinalónga's small neighbouring island, Kalidón, lepers lived a life of exile and isolation

also offer sporting activities, then the resort hotel *Kaliméra Kríti* 1000 m to the east is a good option *(455 rooms | tel. 28 41 06 90 00 | www.kalimerakriti.gr | Expensive)*. For those who like to eat fish, the *Taverna Fisherman's – To Stéki tou Psará (Moderate)* on the coast, east of the fjord, is highly recommended. *22 km (13½ mi)*

SPINALÓNGA ★ ☼
(141 F2–3) (ω O3–4)

Spinalónga is an island north-west of the Gulf of Mirabéllo. *Kalidón* is a small island that lies offshore to the north and it served as a leper colony from 1913–57. The lepers lived in isolation in a village they built them-

mediately taken from their mothers and sent to an orphanage in Crete. Bread and other necessities were brought from Pláka but apart from the sporadic visits of a doctor the lepers had no medical care at all.

The road around the island is 1000 m long. The trip out by excursion boat is worthwhile to experience the sorrow of the island, but also because of the diverse coastal scenery. INSIDER TIP Having an English guide is recommended, the guides bring the past to life with their retelling of the island's history. *Boats from Ágios (12–17 euros) and Eloúnda (10 euros) | entrance 2 euros, guided tour 2 euros*

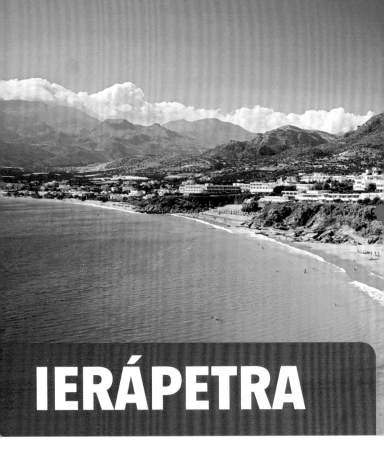

IERÁPETRA

On the radio, Arabic music mixes with Cretan sounds while winds from the south blow in dust from the Sahara. In the centre of old town Ierápetra a minaret towers upwards, there are hints of Africa everywhere in the landscape.

Here tourism plays second fiddle to agriculture which is much more important, as evidenced by the many greenhouses which harness their energy from the sun. A reservoir provides irrigation. Ierápetra and its region is an unusual part of Crete, an area that is completely different from the other regions on the island.

While Ierápetra suffers from the heat during midsummer, it is an ideal holiday destination during the winter so life bustles here throughout the whole year. You can swim in the Libyan Sea even during December and January.

The coastal region of Ierápetra extends up to the Messará Plateau, which borders on the 1231 m (4030 ft) high Asterússia mountain range. The only area developed for tourism is between Mírtos and Makrigialós. The other coastal villages lie far from the main road and are exclusively destinations for independent tourists. The good sandy beaches are concentrated along the coastal strip between Ierápetra and Makrigialós. While bathing paradise can be found on the small is-

Photo: View of Makrígialos

A touch of Africa – greenhouses, mountain villages and lonely beaches – you can winter very well in the warmth of southern Crete

lands of Chrisí and Koufonísi. Both are uninhabited and offer fine sand beaches without hotels. Koufonísi does not even have a taverna.

IERÁPETRA

(141 F6) *(𝄞 O6)* **Ierápetra (pop. 11 700) is the southernmost city in Greece. It is located on a large coastal plain that is covered with greenhouses. Cucumbers and tomatoes determine the rhythm of life here more so than the tourists who mostly stay in the 1500-bed beach hotel Petra Mare.**

For tourists the beach promenade is the heart of the city, this is where the tavernas and cafés are lined up next to each other. Just behind it in the west, is the old town, which connects with the new town in the east with its market hall, public authorities and businesses. Good beaches can be found on both sides of the promenade which is paved with colourful marble and travertine tiles.

OLD TOWN
At the western end of the promenade is the Venetian *fortress* built in 1626 *(Tue–Sun 8.30am–3pm | admission free)*. Behind

Climb to the Venetian fortress and enjoy a beautiful view of the harbour

In antiquity Ierápetra was a settlement known as Hierapytna. At the start of the 4th century it was the seat of a bishopric and later served as a fortress for the Venetians and the Turks. In 1798 Napoleon spent a night here on his way to Egypt. According to legend he went ashore with five sailors to get fresh water for his fleet. He started a conversation with the local notary, who did not recognise him, and with typical Cretan hospitality invited him for dinner and a night's rest. The next morning the notary found a note on his guest's empty bed which revealed his identity.

it, the old town stretches out with its small alleyways that date from the Turkish period. On the quiet square is a mosque with a restored minaret and well house.

ARCHAEOLOGICAL MUSEUM
The small museum in a former Turkish school has ceramics and coins, an especially beautiful Minoan sarcophagus with images of everyday life and a statue of the goddess Persephone dating from the 2nd century AD. Examples of early working techniques are given by two simple pottery wheels and a mould used to make bronze sickles in the Minoan era. *Tue–Sun*

8.30am–3pm | entrance 2 euros | Odós Ethnikís Antistáseos (close to the square in the new town)

FOOD & DRINK

CÁSTRO (O CALLÉS)

An *ouzerí* that offers a wide range of small dishes and a favourite spot for the local fishermen and pensioners. *Daily 5am–midnight | opposite the fort on the coast road | Budget*

INSIDER TIP ► LEVANTE

A well kept restaurant on the promenade that serves excellent food and is also good value for money. Apart from fresh fish, proprietor Níkos also serves a fantastic *moussaká. Daily from 11am | Odós Stratigoú Satouíl 38 | www.ierapetra.net/levante | Budget*

INSIDER TIP ► PÓRTEGO

Bar, café and restaurant in a 100-year old building with a small and atmospheric inner courtyard. Good variety of typical *mesédes. Daily from 7.30pm | Odós N. Foniadáki 8 | Expensive*

SHOPPING

MARKET HALL (AGORÁ)

Meat, fish, fruit and vegetables. *Odós Ethnikís Antistáseos/Odós Kostúla Adrianú*

FRESH MARKET (LAIKÍ AGORÁ)

Every Saturday morning a colourful street market takes place in the east of the city. *Odós Psilináki*

SPORTS

A water sports school on Ierápetra's beach offers dive courses, windsurfing, water-skiing and sailing and canoes and paddle boats can also be hired.

ENTERTAINMENT

Music bars and nightclubs are the feature in the *Odós Kirvá* behind the promenade *(e.g. Seven, Saxo, Insomnia)*. At café *Odeion* (only open during the evening) you can enjoy good wine and delicious snacks in the inner courtyard of a villa *(from 7pm | Odós Lasthénous 18 | Moderate)*. 5 km (3 mi) inland in the village of *Vaínia* in the *Ouzeri Plátanos (closed Mon)* on the village square you can join the locals under the mulberry trees for wine and Cretan *mesédes*.

WHERE TO STAY

INSIDER TIP ► CRETAN VILLA

This small two-storey guest house with a tiny inner courtyard was built during the 19th century and was once the town's first hospital. Its proprietor, a true local patriot, has decorated it in Cretan style and takes good care of his guests. *9 rooms | Odós Oplárchu Lakérda 16A | tel. 28 42 02 85 22 | www.cretan-villa.gr | Moderate*

★ **Áno Viánnos**
Visit the young icon painter and the old church in this large mountain village
→ p. 88

★ **Chrisí Island**
Swim like Robinson Crusoe: on a beach lover's dream island
→ p. 88

★ **Kapsá Monastery**
A monastery in a lovely setting on a cliff over the south coast, with a local healer said to be a miracle worker
→ p. 89

MARCO POLO HIGHLIGHTS

EROTOKRITOS

An idyllically located house in the old town with 5 rooms, some of them with kitchenettes. The proprietor Evangélia shows real Cretan hospitality. *Párodos Stratigú Satuíl | tel. 28 42 02 81 51 | Budget*

PETRA MARE

A hotel block that can be seen from afar, but it is nevertheless a very pleasant place to stay. A pedestrian promenade leads into the town centre about 800 m further, while to the east is a long pebble beach. If at all possible, book a room with a sea view! *Coastal road east of the centre | tel. 28 42 02 33 41 | www.petramare.com | Moderate*

WHERE TO GO

ÁNO VIÁNNOS ⭐ (140 C5) (*M5*)

This large mountain village with 1100 inhabitants is a favourite stopover between Ierápetra and Iráklio. In the main road close to the village church, you can watch the young icon painter and restorer Emmanuíl Psarákis at work during the late mornings. Signs in the main road show the way to the Byzantine church *Agía Pelagía* with frescoes dating back to around 1360 *(open irregularly)*. *36 km (22 mi)*

CHRISÍ ISLAND ⭐ (142 A6) (*O7*)

Chrisí is a dream island for beach lovers. Besides a taverna, a beach bar and dunes

above which the bizarre roots and branches of the 10 m (33 ft) high trees tower, there is also long sandy beaches. Excursion and taxi boats travel daily from Ierápetra during the summer. Staying overnight is prohibited, but many young Greeks do not adhere to this rule – probably because there is no police station. Nude bathing is as common as partying on the beach at night.

SEE YOU TOMORROW

Buses, ships and planes keep to the official schedules but in everyday Cretan life, punctuality is not a necessity. Cretans seldom arrange to meet at an exact time, but prefer to be vague with

áwrio = tomorrow , *to proí* = morning , *to apógewma* = afternoon (from about 4pm) or *to wrádi* = at night (from about 8pm). If you as a guest accept this trait you will save yourself a lot of trouble.

Stopover in Áno Viánnos and visit the local icon painter

EPISKOPÍ (141 F5) *(Ⓜ P5)*

The little village on the main road to the northern coast has a very interesting church, *Ágios Geórgios kai Charálambos*. The double church dates back to the 12th/13th century and impresses with its tambour and beautiful arcade structure. Can only be viewed from the outside. *10 km (6 mi)*

KAPSÁ MONASTERY ★ ♨
(143 D4) *(Ⓜ Q5)*

This monastery, which is partially built into a cliff, was built during the 15th century and its beautiful setting makes it worth a visit. John the Baptist and Josíf Gerondojánnis – a miracle healer during the 19th century – are both honoured here *(daily 9am–12.30pm and 4–7pm)*. You can have a lovely picnic beneath the monastery or swim at the sandy beach under the shade of old tamarisks. In the

village of *Kaló Neró*, 2000 m west on the road to Ierápetra, the friendly and quaint taverna *Oásis* invites you to sample their snacks and *rakí*. Occasionally they also serve *kounélli krassáto*, rabbit in red wine sauce *(Budget)*. In the distance on the far eastern side of the southern coast you can see the small village of Goudourás. It looks like a city, but is made up almost entirely of greenhouses. It is not worth a visit. *46 km (29 mi)*

KERATÓKAMBOS (140 C6) *(Ⓜ M6)*

A coastal village that is popular amongst backpackers. The sandy beach to the east of the village is a good place to sunbathe in the dunes. *48 km (30 mi)*

KOUFONÍSI (143 E5) *(Ⓜ R6)*

An island that is at times completely deserted, its fine sand and flat beaches are uninhabited. During the summer you can take a boat trip daily from 10am from Makrigialós to the island. The trip takes about an hour. In the bay where the boat anchors, you will see the ruins of a theatre and homes of a Roman settlement from around the time of Christ's birth. The island was once famous for the purple dye derived from sea snails.

LÉNDAS �►
(139 D6) (*ɰ J6*)

This coastal village which is popular amongst independent travellers and campers only has a few houses and tavernas. The whitewashed houses are surrounded by beautiful flower gardens and there is a short sand and pebble beach in front of the village. A 15 minute walk further brings you to a sandy beach where nude bathing is common.

Léndas is built on the site of the ancient city of *Levin* and once was the harbour for *Górtys* and during that time there were

also some thermal springs. There are also the Roman remains of an Askelopios shrine dating back to the 2nd century. The early Christian basilica was built during the 5th/6th century *(Tue–Sun 9am–3pm | admission free)*.

Stay in the laid back **INSIDER TIP** *Lentas Bungalows*, where the proprietors speak English. A communal kitchen is available to guests. There are 12 rooms in the five houses and using the air conditioning costs extra. *(tel. 28 92 09 52 21 | www. lentas-online.com | Budget)*. One of the most beautiful restaurants on the entire southern coast the **INSIDER TIP** *Taverna Greco (www.lentas-elgreco.com | Moderate)* serves excellent dishes on its flower-filled terrace right by the sea. *90 km (56 mi)*

MAKRÍGIALOS
(142 C4) (*ɰ Q5*)

Makrígialos (and *Análipsis* which adjoins it in the east) paints a pretty picture for beach lovers. And with its long flat sandy beaches and lots of shade it is ideal for families with small children. In the centre of Makrígialos, close to the village church, lies the foundations of an ancient Roman villa from the 1st century (with free access). Just outside the village in the direction of Ierápetra a sign shows the way to the remains of a late Minoan villa.

To Stéki tou Miná/Mina's Place (Moderate) is an atmospheric fish taverna right next to the harbour. You can have a lovely stay in the **INSIDER TIP** *White River Cottages* in a narrow, very green valley about 1000 m from the coast *(13 rooms | tel. 28 43 05 11 20 | www.attika.de | Moderate)*. Refurbished labourer's cottages with stone floors and wooden decks are available to rent. They are decorated in true Cretan style. There is a small pool in the centre of the valley. The path to the village and the beach is very dark at night, so a torch is a necessity. *24 km (15 mi)*

LOW BUDGET

▶ Everybody along the promenade on the island of Chrisí wants to make money from the excursion boats. Tickets for the trip are sold on the boat, at travel agencies and tavernas. The competition is fierce but that means that families or small groups can negotiate prices under 25 euros.

▶ Outside of the peak season, the coastal villages west of Ierápetra offer rooms from 20 euros, like *Gorgóna (tel. 28 95 07 13 53)* in Àrvi or *Venetía (tel. 28 91 09 22 58)* in Tsoútsouros.

Makrígialos is ideal for holidays with small children: lots of shady trees

MÍRTOS 🌊 (141 D6) (*⑳ N6*)

A former hippie village on the edge of orange and lemon groves offers a long pebbled beach and isolated swimming bays. Travellers come here to spend peaceful holidays swimming during the day and sitting in the small rustic tavernas at night. Close to the village, on the hills of *Foúrnu Kórfi* and *Pírgos*, archaeologists have uncovered the remains of an early Minoan villa with about 90 rooms and a double storey building. Both sites are open to visitors and can be reached by following the signs on the coastal road towards Ierápetra. It is only possible to get there on foot and the ascent starts directly at the signpost. *15 km (9¼ mi)*

PÉFKI (142 C4) (*⑳ Q5*)

The unspoiled mountain village Péfki which is situated about 4 km from Makrígialos,

is a good destination for those staying in this region for a few days. It has old buildings, lots of flowers and two quaint tavernas *Weinlaube (Budget)* and *Piperiá (Budget)* in the village centre. *28 km (17 mi)*

BRAMIANÁ RESERVOIR
(141 E5) (*⑳ O5*)

Built in 1986 this reservoir at Gra Ligiá has a capacity for 16 million litres of water and is the largest in Crete. It irrigates the many greenhouses in the region. During the winter it is a bird paradise with more than 200 species of birds. They include spotted eagles, snake eagles, peregrine falcons, bitterns, herons and pink flamingos and ibis. You can hike around the whole reservoir and there are observation points for amateur ornithologists. *5 km (3 mi)*

SITÍA

On its far eastern side Crete transforms itself yet again. The countryside becomes lovelier, the olive groves thin out and the mountains are not so dominant. The roads wind through the valleys which stretch from the interior to the coast. Villages are isolated and wind generators dot the mountains and its stony plateaus.

Even the mentality of the people here seems to be different: there are no bullet holes in the road signs, indicating that the Cretan resistance to foreign rule is no longer an issue here. But the sound of the *lýra* can still be heard, especially at festivals, where the instrument lies ready for use in many a taverna.

The region is still undiscovered by mass tourism and only Sitía, in the lively centre of the region, has a large hotel. There are only a few beaches but they are very long and – apart from Vái which is popular with day visitors – always have lots of space. There are only a few historical sites and the Minoan palace of Káto Zákros sees more turtles than visitors. This is a region of beautiful nature and scenic landscapes.

SITÍA

(143 D2) *(ऒ Q4)* **This small, friendly, country town (pop. 8200) stretches over**

Palm trees, lemons, raisins – in spring the air smells of herbs, in autumn the grapes are pressed – Crete's east is still pristine

a broad low hillside in the south-west corner of the bay.

Many streets run at right angles to each other, giving Sitía a feeling of order that other Cretan towns lack. The road along the coast starts at a nice sandy beach in the east and leads you around the harbour. Fishing boats and yachts moor along the centre pier while the outer piers are reserved for freight ships and ferries. Where

the road turns towards the north, is Platía Iróon Politechníu the central square with its palm trees and cafés which is the ideal place to soak up the atmosphere of the town.

All the important shops and tavernas lie in the parallel alleys around Odós El. Venizélou and Odós Vitséndzou Kornárou and the cross streets that lead uphill. The castle is the only historical sight worth

Fishing boats in Sitiá harbour: well kept and colourful

visiting. Sitía is still a very young town: the medieval settlement was completely abandoned after the Turks destroyed it in 1651 and was only reoccupied in 1871. Most of the houses in the old town date back to the last century.

SIGHTSEEING

ARCHAEOLOGICAL MUSEUM

The museum is housed in one hall and on display are items from 22 excavation sites in the region (mostly without written explanations). One particularly fine exhibit is the 30 cm high male ivory torso with stylized hair made from golden bronze. The Minoan grape press is also very interesting. *Tue–Sun 8.30am–3pm | entrance 2 euros | at the town exit on the road towards Ierápetra*

FORTRESS

A former Venetian fortress named *Kazárma* where theatre and concert performances are held during the summer. *Open irregularly | admission free*

FOLK MUSEUM

Interesting collection of Cretan furniture, costumes, embroidery and weaving in original Cretan surroundings. *Mon–Sat 10am–1pm | entrance 2 euros | Odós Kapetán Sifí 26 (close to the harbour square)*

FOOD & DRINK

BALKÓNI/BALCONY

This restaurant is on the upper floor of a house from the 19th century. It is cheerfully furnished and serves creative Greek dishes made from regional and organic products. Guests who want a drink at the bar are also welcome. Wine per bottle only. *Daily from 6pm | Odós Kazantzákis/corner Odós Funtalídu | www.balcony-restaurant.com* | Expensive

O MÍCHOS

Taverna on the promenade. Proprietor Michális is very proud of his chicken dishes. During October he also serves stuffed squid but does not list it on the menu. *Daily noon–4pm and from 6pm | Odós K. Karamanlí* | Budget

SPRING OF PARADISE

The best taverna in Sitía lies 15 km (9¼ mi) outside of the town on the way to Ierápetra (143 D3) (Q5). Here you can sit underneath vines and fruit trees close to the spring and enjoy the best potatoes in Crete as well as other traditional Cretan dishes. The spring water tastes as good

as the wine. *Daily from 11am | Drapaní Sykiás | tel. 28 43 03 14 05 | Moderate*

SHOPPING

SITIAKÁ GLIKA
Owner Anna Garefaláki specialises in products from the region including cakes, wines, *oúzo* and *rakí*. *Odós Em. Russelláki 17*

SPORTS & LEISURE

The town of Sitía itself is not recommended as a holiday destination for sports enthusiasts. The next water sport centre is about 25 km (15 mi) further in Vái. You can swim on the sandy beach (which has no shade) east of the town's edge. It lies just beneath the very busy main road in the direction of Vái.

Távli is a favourite game not only in Sitía but throughout Crete

rock and international hits. *700 m from the outskirts on the bypass road from the ferry to the airport*

ENTERTAINMENT

There is no shortage of bars and clubs in Sitía. Yet the locals prefer to spend their evenings in the tavernas outside of the town with real Cretan live music.

ROÚSSA EKKLISÍA
(143 E3) (*ØD R4*)
In the centre of this village, almost 9 km (5½ mi) above Sitía, Níkos and Nifikúla run a simple taverna under some trees and serve Cretan dishes and homemade wines from the barrel. At night, when driving back to Sitía the reflections of the lights of the town look like diamonds glittering in the ocean.

PLANETARION CLUB
Sitía's dance club, open every weekend during midsummer but otherwise only sporadically. Because there are no houses in the vicinity, the music is usually turned up full volume even in the open air section. The DJs love to play both Greek

WHERE TO STAY

Sitía only has one large hotel, the *Sitia Beach*. Apart from that there are modern town hotels, private rooms and small

⭐ **Chamési**
A Minoan villa with a view → **p. 97**

⭐ **Káto Zakrós**
Between a beach and a rocky wilderness lies a Minoan palace → **p. 98**

⭐ **Vái**
Crete's famous palm grove beach → **p. 100**

⭐ **Xerókambos**
Beautiful, undiscovered beaches → **p. 101**

MARCO POLO HIGHLIGHTS

guest houses and holiday houses in the vicinity.

INSIDER TIP ARCHONTIKÓ

This is a guest house in a 100-year old restored mansion in the old town. It has a lovely communal terrace where you can prepare your own breakfast. Here you stay in a street amongst locals so you feel like a local yourself. The proprietor prefers not to have a website, because she likes to handle bookings personally over the telephone. *11 rooms, 10 of them with shared bathrooms | Odos I. Kondiláki 16 | tel. 28 43 02 81 72 | Budget*

LOW BUDGET

▶ You can eat very inexpensively at *Stéki*, a taverna in Sitías where a half a litre of wine only costs 2 euros and spaghetti with grilled chicken only 4 euros (no cover charge!). Inside you can have a comfortable seat close to the television or outside with the locals on the green pavement next to the road *(daily from 10am | Odós Papandréou 7 | Budget)*.

▶ You can team up with others and travel inexpensively on Crete. When taking a taxi from the airport to the city (or any other destination) get together with some other tourists and pretend to know each other. A taxi driver will charge just once if passengers know one another but will charge each one the full price if they don't know one another. A short discussion with other waiting passengers will do the trick!

ELYSEE

A chic modern hotel directly on the pedestrian promenade. Parking at the back of the hotel. *26 rooms | K. Karamanlí 14 | tel. 28 43 02 23 12 | www.elysee-hotel.gr | Budget*

SITÍA BEACH

This is the only large hotel in the region. It has no less than three freshwater pools, tennis courts, and a spa and fitness centre. The sea and beach is on the opposite side of the road (free beach towels for hotel guests) while the town centre and the bus terminal are only 5 minutes away. *161 rooms | Odós K. Karamanlí | tel. 28 43 02 88 21 | www.sitiabeach.com | Expensive*

INFORMATION

TOURIST INFORMATION
Leofóros Karamanlí/corner Odós Papandréou | tel. 28 41 02 42 00

WHERE TO GO

AGÍA FOTIÁ
(143 E2–3) (*ΔΩ R4*)

In the fields below the village archaeologists have excavated an early Minoan cemetery with a large number of shaft graves and tomb chambers. An archaeological site signpost shows the way. Continue about 250 m on the dirt road until you reach the fenced in excavation site on the low INSIDER TIP *Kouphóta hill* with ruins of an early Minoan settlement. The site which is funded by the EU is very well organised but closed due to a lack of guards and the fence is not always respected by curious tourists.

In the village centre, the attractive *Taverna Nerómilos (Moderate)* which is only open at night is situated next to an old watermill. *7 km (4 mi)*

The countryside in the east of Crete is full of peaceful olive groves

CHAMÉSI ★ ☀
(142 C3) (*Ø Q4*)

On a hilltop south-east of this traditional mountain village are the foundation walls from the only oval shaped *estate* from Minoan times *(admission free)*. You can enjoy a magnificent view across the land and sea from a field full of fennel, aromatic thyme, sage and oregano. To get there go from the western end of the village, turn off to the left beneath the remains of two windmills onto a dirt track that goes for about 700 m to the excavation site. *10 km (6 mi)*

CHANDRÁS PLATEAU
(143 D4) (*Ø Q–R5*)

In Epáno Episkopí (between Sitía and Ierápetra) is a tarmac road marked Zíros that leads through Néa Presós on the plateau, a centre for Crete's sultana cultivation. The villages are still very traditional and the *kafenía* cheap. North of Chandrás you can explore the remains of the abandoned village *Woíla,* the seat of a Venetian royal family, who later converted Islam. In the chapel of the hamlet a fresco above a medieval tomb shows Mary with baby Jesus with the dead man's family wearing traditional 16th century dress. The small fresco next to it depicts a young girl on her deathbed. In the hamlet of *Etiá* is a well preserved Venetian palace that dates to the 15th century.

Good food and accommodation can be found in the only taverna in Chandrás, the ☺ *Lemon Tree (Moderate)* run by British chef Mark Cardnell. He creatively refines Cretan recipes and works mainly with regional produce, it is also popular with the locals. *30 km (18½ mi)*

When you leave Sitía on the road to Iráklio, after about 2000 m a narrow road turns to the right with a Agion Panton Gorge signpost. The road goes for 8 km (5 mi) through the countryside to the sea and then runs parallel to a gorge for 2000 m to a small hamlet. The hamlet is only inhabited during the summer for the olive and grape harvest but it has a small taverna which is open all year *(Budget)*. On a terrace high above the gorge is an abandoned monastery. The small convent, which dates back to approx. the 15th century is situated in an idyllic position above the gorge. In the sooty remains of the church arches are some frescoes dating back to the 17th century. *6 km (3¾ mi)*

The ruins of two early Christian basilicas are all that remain of the ancient city with the same name. The simple, small African-looking houses rise from the dunes dotted with dry Cretan date palms. From the ⛱ sandy beach with its crystal clear waters, the view stretches as far as Cape Síderos, the north-eastern tip of Crete, which the military has unfortunately claimed for itself. No deckchairs on the beach and not a single hotel in sight for miles. Ítanos is a the perfect alternative to the busy beach very close to the palm tree lined beach of Vái! *25 km (15 mi)*

KÁTO ZÁKROS ⭐ (143 F4) (*M R5*)

Archaeologists have been excavating four Minoan palaces on the island since 1962.

Dolce vita in Crete: eating under the trees on Káto Zákros beach

There are an estimated 300 rooms. It is situated in the small green coastal plain and was the only Cretan palace that was not pillaged. Its construction was based on the same layout as the other Minoan palaces. Of interest is the bronze foundry left of the central courtyard and the plastered washbasin in a room which may have been the throne room some 3500 years ago. Children will enjoy the many large tortoises which sun themselves between the old walls (Tue–Sun 10am–5pm | entrance 3 euros).

There are many tavernas along the adjoining pebble beach of Káto Zákros and there are also rooms to let that are right on the beach. For a longer stay opt for INSIDER TIP Stella's Traditional Apartments. They are part of a very nice bungalow development run by the Ailamákis siblings. The development comprises 13 flats and a magical garden about 500 m from the beach in the midst of a rather desolate landscape (tel. 28 43 02 37 39 | www.stelapts.com | Moderate). Stella's husband Ilías (who has climbed Mont Blanc and written a book about bodybuilding) guides mountain hikes and climbs, in the region. Free of charge for guests and 10 euros for others. 45 km (28 mi)

INSIDER TIP MÓCHLOS
(142 B–C3) (*Q P4*)

2000 m outside of the village, which lies in a lonely plain beneath the northern coastal road, holidaymakers enjoy themselves in a French holiday club. They seldom venture into the village which means that the fishing village has retained its character. The tavernas on the coast, opposite the small island of Móchlos with the ruins of an early Minoan settlement and necropolis, invite you to while away some time. There are small sand and pebble beaches about 5–15 minutes by foot

to the west of the village. Enjoy good food in the taverna Ta Kavoúria at the harbour. Fish and lobster are relatively affordable. The proprietor Spíro Galanákis also rents out 11 reasonably priced rooms in the village (tel. 28 43 09 42 04 | Budget) and arranges trips to the island. 30 km (18½ mi)

NÉA PRESÓS
(143 D3) (*Q Q5*)

About a mile outside this peaceful village on the way to Sitía, are the remains of the ancient city of Presós, which dates back to the 12th century BC. The Eteocretans were here even before the time of the Greek Dorians. What remains of the city is the foundations of a temple, the walls of a Hellenic house and a few scattered stone blocks. More impressive than the ruins is the experience of silence and solitude in the midst of beautiful natural surroundings. 16 km (10 mi)

PALÉKASTRO (143 F2) (*Q R4*)

Palékastro was founded in 1850 and is very popular amongst independent travellers because of its proximity to a large number of good, quiet beaches. At ● Chióna beach archaeologists have uncovered the ruins of the second largest Minoan city in Crete. This city experienced a boom during 155–1220 BC, it covered an area of about 12 acres and had a well designed canal system (Tue–Sun 8.30am–3pm | admission free | follow the sign to Rousolako from the road to the beach).

At the northern beach end of Chiónas you will have the best views from two tavernas Chióna and Bátis, their terraces are right on the sea and look out towards the far Orient. A good place to enjoy some fish (both daily from noon | Expensive). At the square of Palékastro visit the restaurant Hellas (daily from 8am | Budget) which is traditional and unpretentious. At night it is the meeting place for locals and tourists alike. Opposite the restaurant is the *Tourist Information*, which can help you find a room or holiday home *(Mon–Sat 9am–1pm and 6–8.30pm, in summer daily 9am–9.30pm | tel. 28 43 06 12 25 | www.palaikastro.com)*. Blending well into the surrounding landscape is the hotel INSIDERTIP *Marína Village* with 32 rooms with own garden and pool. The beach and the town can be reached by foot within 15 minutes *(tel. 28 43 06 12 84 | www.palaikastro.com/marinavillage | Moderate)*. 24 km (15 mi)

PETRÁS (143 D2) (*Q4*)

About a mile from the hamlet of Petrás, lie the remains of the Hellenic city *Tripitós (free access)*. On the rocky ridge on which Petrás is built archaeologists have found the walls of a Minoan palace *(also freely accessible)*. 2 km (1¼ mi)

THRIPTÍ (142 B4) (*P5*)

Vines are cultivated here just below the 1476 m (4850 ft) high *Afendís Kawússi* in a landscape which is reminiscent of the tea plantations in the Indian and Sri Lankan highlands. Vintners live here from summer until autumn and here Crete shows another one of its unique sides. You can reach Thriptí by a forest road from *Káto Chorió* and from here you can drive across the mountains and peaks to *Orinó* with its many threshing floors and carob trees, through untouched mountain villages like *Skinokápsala* and *Ágios Jánnis*, to reach the southern coast at *Koutsounári*. 50 km (31 mi) to Thriptí, 70 km (43 mi) to the coast

TÓPLOU MONASTERY ●
(143 E2) (*R4*)

This fortress-like monastery high on a plateau has a *church* and *museum* with valuable icons and frescoes, copper etchings and wood carvings from the 14th century. A certain Johannes Kornáros painted the valuable icons in the church during 1770. They illustrate miniature stories from the text of an ode dating back to the 7th century *(daily 9am–1pm and 2–pm | entrance 2.50 euros)*. The *kafenío* next door offers refreshments. 21 km (13 mi)

VÁI ★ (143 F2) (*R4*)

The beach at the edge of the former palm grove (which is closed to the public) is very overcrowded, but worth a visit to see the unique landscape. There is a fee to

park, a taverna *(Budget)* and a water sports centre. *25 km (15 mi)*

XERÓKAMBOS ★
(143 E4) (*M R5*)

Xerókambos has only been accessible by car since 2000 which is when the tarmac road was built. This is a secret hideaway for people who prefer quiet beaches and there are many of them here: small hidden bays in the east and the 500 m long wide sandy *Ámbelos beach* on the south coast. There are a few isolated tavernas and guest houses and no umbrellas to rent. Between the two beaches archaeologists have uncovered the ruins of a Hellenic settlement next to the St Nikolas chapel. *43 km (26 mi)*

ZÁKROS
(143 F4) (*M R5*)

At the edge of this mountain village (after Káto Zákros) the road to cuts through a villa that dates back to the Neo-Palatial period. From Zákros you can hike for about two hours through the Valley of the Dead to the Minoan palace of Káto Zákros. The valley is lush and green and the walls are full of caves where people were buried until the early Christian period. The way into the valley is signposted from the square of Zákros. *37 km (23 mi)*

Behind fortress-like walls, the Tóplou Monastery houses valuable icons and frescoes

TRIPS & TOURS

The tours are marked in green in the road atlas, pull-out map and on the back cover

RÉTHIMNO'S HINTERLAND: NATURE AND HISTORY

The focus of this trip through the Réthimno hinterland is the landscape of the countryside. You will also learn more about important national monuments, local handcrafts, traditional tavernas and an ancient city. Duration of the round trip to and from Réthimno: approx. 100 km (62 mi) and about 7 hours by car.

Réthimno → p. 47 take the coastal road and at Plataniás turn off at the signpost to Arkádi monastery. The first detour trip is just before Ádele. The detour will take you to the old Venetian village of Marulás, where foreigners have bought and beautifully restored some of the many historical houses.

After strolling through the village you can return to the main road, which continues uphill through several villages before leading through a very narrow valley. Quite suddenly you will find yourself on a plateau with the isolated Arkádi Monastery → p. 55, where you should take at least an hour to sightsee.

From the monastery, a tarmac road leads towards Eléftherna. The road crosses over the plateau and there are numerous points along the way that offer fantastic

Photo: Melidóni's stalactite caves

Journey through Crete's most beautiful areas: the dramatic west, the tranquil east and the spectacular natural beauty of its interior

views of Arkádi and its surroundings. The road continues through the lonely landscape with its grazing sheep and goats on to the village of Eléftherna which has four traditional coffee houses where you can also have something to eat. The highest mountain of the island, Psilorítis, is ☀ visible from here. Eléftherna has about 250 inhabitants and is 400 m (1300 ft) above sea level.

Further on, you will reach the neighbouring village of INSIDER TIP Archéa Eléftherna, which is situated in the area of the ancient city of Eléftherna. Systematic excavations started there in 1985 and every summer scientists from the University of Crete carry out further excavations. Drive out from the village square down to taverna I Akropolis from here you can explore the ancient sites. A 10 minute walk along the remains of the old city wall and you reach two massive cisterns, carved from the rocks about 2300 years ago. You will reach another excavation area if you follow the Ancient Eleutherna signposts from the road leading to Margarítes.

The road now heads steadily downwards until you reach the old national road, which until the 1980s was the only road that connected Réthimno and Iráklio. From here you turn right towards Pérama where you turn left towards the coast.

Sandbanks: in good weather you can walk across to the little island of Elafonísi

Margarítes → p. 55 is the next destination. Here, on right hand side of the road you can visit the first potter's workshop to see how the man-sized *pithoi* vessels are produced. Many other ceramic workshops have pottery that is easier to carry home as a memento. Margarítes has two equally good tavernas, both on the square and they are both worth a worth a visit. There are other tavernas on the street at the lower end of the town.

Go over a narrow bridge (the river only flows during the winter) and turn right after the bridge to Melidóni. Just before you reach the village, you can visit an olive oil press on the right hand side where you can also buy good quality olive oil → p. 56. From the village square you can drive a few kilometres in the direction of Agía where there are numerous charcoal kilns in operation. Have a rest in Melidóni's village square before you take the road to the Melidóni stalactite cave → p. 56. After Melidóni you will finally reach the sleepy hamlet of Exándis. Turn right and you will be on the new national road that will take you back to Réthimno or Iráklio.

2 ON YOUR WAY – IN THE WILD WEST

A day of winding roads – still untouched by tourism – awaits you in the west and south-west of the island, where on occasion you can also swim and go for hikes. Some of the roads are unsurfaced but you do not need an off-road vehicle. This round trip starts and ends in Chaniá: 230 km (143 mi), minimum time 12–14 hours.

To leave Chaniá → p. 33 follow the signposts inland to Ómalos and to Samaría Gorge and pass through Agiá, notorious during the Second World War as a German military prison. Cretan resistance fighters as well as German soldiers were tortured and executed here. In Foúrnes, leave the main road and head towards Néa Roúmata. From here the route leads through thick forested mountains towards the south. The chestnut trees are especially beautiful during the autumn. They are lined up along the underground water seams. At the southern end of Agía Iríni you can take a short hike through the upper section of the Iríni Gorge → p. 42. This short stretch is enough to show you the beauty of the gorge. In the next village, Epanochóri, which only has 40 inhabitants, has some rustic cafés on the main road where you can take a rest.

From Rodováni you can continue to Temeniá and from there an unsurfaced road takes you to Azogirés with its caves. Here the proprietor of the INSIDER TIP▶ Alfa Café on the main road will happily provide you with information about the caves and other activities in the area. Once back on the tarmac road you will soon arrive in Paleochóra → p. 44 on the Libyan Sea. Here you can eat in one of the many tavernas, swim at one of the many beaches and even stay the night. Leave Paleochóra on the road that runs parallel to the sandy beach but turn right towards the mountains before the end of the village. Go through Kondokinígi and Voutás continuing towards Stróvles. 6 km (3¾ mi) further along is Élos, Crete's chestnut growing region where you can take a break, shortly after Élos you will reach the west coast.

After swimming in the South Seas-like beach at Elafonísi → p. 40 you can then visit the Chrisoskalítissa Monastery → p. 40, before you return via Élos and Topólia on the northern coast. Pass Kolimbári and Máleme → p. 43 with its military cemetery, then you reach the motorway and the exit to Chaniá.

3 IN THE EAST: PEACEFUL VILLAGES, SMALL TOWNS

The holiday resorts on Crete's so-called 'Costa Turistica' between Iráklio and Ágios Nikólaos are only one aspect of this multifaceted island. This trip takes you to the east of the island, to the Libyan Sea and Crete's mountains. Duration of the round trip to and from Ágios Nikólaos: 180 km (112 mi). Minimum time 10–12 hours.

During the first hour of the trip, the ever changing view of the Gulf of Mirabéllo is fascinating. Then the road turns inland and you pass the excavations of the Minoan city Goúrnia → p. 79, whose inhabitants enjoyed the view of the gulf 3500 years ago. A few kilometres beyond Pachiá Ámmos the road leads up the mountain.

For the next hour, the road winds upwards along the coast. There is a beautiful view of ⊰⊱ Plátanos from this height. The white slopes are now a gypsum mine. The route meanders through little mountain villages to Chamési → p. 97. Shortly before the village entrance a signpost on the right shows the way to the ⊰⊱ ruins of a Minoan country house, where you will have a panoramic view from the top of the hilltop. From Chamési the road goes down to the harbour town of Sitía → p. 92. Take a stroll along the harbour and through the market alleys and enjoy the atmosphere of the town. A visit to the archaeological museum is also worthwhile.

If you start early enough, you can make a two-hour detour to the Chandrás Plateau → p. 97 and visit Chandrás, Arméni, Etiá and Woíla. It is especially scenic during September. Grapes hang on the vines and are laid out on the street, turning into sweet sultanas in the sun. During a good year, the Chandrás Plateau produces some 600 tonnes of sultanas. At Makrígialos Análipsis → p. 90 you have reached the Libyan Sea where you can have a lovely swim at the child-friendly, sandy Análipsis beach.

As you drive the views alternate between the sea and the peaks of the Thriptí Mountains en route to Ierápetra → p. 85, the unique Cretan town on the south coast. Take some time to stroll through the old town with its mosque and the beach promenade with its cafés and tavernas and then head back to the north coast.

If you run out of time you can take the direct route that runs over the narrowest part of Crete. If you have at least two more hours, the stretch through the foothills of the Lassíthi Mountains is a more interesting option.

If you choose that route, leave Ierápetra and turn off towards Bramianá → p. 91. Pass Crete's largest reservoir (it supplies the

water to the greenhouses around Ierápetra) the road travels uphill to the mountain village Kalamáfka which is 450 m above sea level and has rocks that are quite bizarre. There are 1700 inhabitants in the village. From the town square 225 steps lead to the ⊰⊱ Timíu Stavroú chapel, which crowns a very steep rock. The view from this rock is breathtaking.

In the INSIDER TIP ► *Taverna Kastélos* in the village square, the mother still does the cooking while her son Geórgios makes his own *rakí* and socialises with to the guests *(daily from 9am | Budget)*. If you make this a quick stop, you can still visit the neighbouring village of Prína and spend the afternoon in true Cretan style, at in the taverna *Pitopolus (daily from 10 am | Budget)* where Dímitris the proprietor, regularly plays his *lýra*. You now need another half an hour to reach Ágios Nikólaos → p. 73.

Prime location: the site of the 3500-year old Minoan city of Goúrnia

4 HIKE THROUGH CRETE'S GRANDIOSE SAMARIÁ GORGE

The ⭐ Samariá Gorge in the White Mountains is the longest in Europe at 18 km (11 mi). The hike from the Ómalos Plateau down to the Libyan Sea is almost 14 km (8½ mi) long and takes about 4–5 hours to complete, sturdy shoes are a necessity. The gorge is closed between mid/end October until start/mid May due to the danger of rock falls. During the summer hikes through the gorge, that include travel to and from holiday resorts, are arranged everywhere on the island. Entrance: 5 euros.

The hike starts 1229 m (4032 ft) above sea level at Xylóskla, where steps lead you into the gorge. This is also where the White Mountains National Park Information Centre has all the information about the nature and conservation rules of the gorge. The steps lead to the view of the 2080 m (6824 ft) high Gíngilos for about an hour through woods down to the bottom of the gorge with its rushing stream. You will reach the abandoned village of Samariá with a drinking fountain, emergency service station and toilets. The last inhabitants left in 1962 when the gorge was declared a national park. Further on the gorge narrows even more until it is only 3–4 m wide at the so-called 'iron gates'. Shortly afterwards you will reach the coastal plain, from where you need to walk 3 km (1¾ mi) in the heat towards the coastal hamlet of Agía Rouméli with many tavernas, a few guest houses and a long pebble beach. From here, a boat travels to Chóra Sfakíon, where buses depart for Chaniá, Réthimno and Iráklio.

SPORTS & ACTIVITIES

Just like many other islands, Crete is an El Dorado for water sports fans but it also offers hikers and mountain climbers a challenge with its high mountains and deep gorges. Things are not always well organised so in many cases improvisation is the order of the day.

BUNGEE JUMPING

A INSIDER TIP bungee jump at Arádena, near the south coast, take a lot of bravery. You can dive 138 m (450 ft) from the bridge into the Arádena Gorge while vultures circle above *(Liquidbungy | June–Aug Fri–Sun from noon | 100 euros |* *Arádena | tel. 69 37 61 51 91 | www.bungy. gr)*. There is also the option of a more moderate drop from a crane at the water resort *Star Beach* at Chersónisos on the eastern edge of the town. The drop is only 50 m (160 ft) which also allows for tandem jumps *(Star Beach Bungee | daily from 10am | approx. 50 euros | Chersónisos | www.starbeach.gr)*.

DIVING

Cretan diving sites are particularly suited to beginners due to their crystal clear water, good centres and interesting underwater rock formations. However, there

Photo: Across the Lassíthi Plateau by bicycle

From the sedate to the spectacular: water sports and hiking enthusiasts will be spoiled for choice

are very few fish to be seen. In Crete archaeologists also have a say in the choice of dive sites as they fear that divers will disturb excavations and even smuggle pieces out of the country.

A few diving schools (some also offer introductory courses for adults and children):

– ● *Atlantis Diving Centre (Aquila Réthimno beach | Ádele)* and in the

Grecotel Club Marine Palace (Panórmo | tel. 28 31 07 16 40 | www.atlantis-creta. com/home)

– *Creta Maris Dive Centre (Liménas Chersónisou | Hotel Creta Maris | tel. 28 97 02 21 22 | www.dive-cretamaris. gr)*

– *Dive Together (on the coast road | Plakiás | tel. 28 32 03 23 13 | www.crete. dive2gether.com)*

– INSIDER TIP Notos Mare *(at the new harbour | Chóra Sfakíon | tel. 28 25 09 13 33 | www.notosmare.com)*

FISHING

No permits are required to fish from the coast and fishing lines and lures are available in all coastal villages.

GOLF

Crete's 18-hole golf course, *The Crete Golf Club*, was opened in 2003, 7 km (4¼ mi) from Chersónisos *(on the Chersónisos–Kastélli road | tel. 28 97 02 60 00 | www.crete-golf.com)*. There is also a 9-hole golf course with two playing options, on the grounds of the *Porto Eloúnda* hotel in Eloúnda *(tel. 28 41 04 19 03 | www.porto elounda.gr)*.

HIKING

The E4 European long distance hiking trail stretches from the west to the east coast of Crete. You should allow four weeks for the complete hike. The signposting is good but not perfect. Fitness is essential because you will be crossing mountains and a tent would also be useful.

You can also undertake many hikes on Crete on your own or you can also book one or two-week hikes through specialist travel agencies in Crete. If you are planning multiple day hikes through the mountains, you should contact the Cretan Mountaineering Society which also offer huts in the White Mountains and in the Ída Mountains. They also organise weekend guided hikes. The Mountaineering Club of Iráklio publish their programme in English on the internet. *www.interkriti. org/orivatikos/orivat.html*

Special travel agencies: *Happy Walker (Odós Tombázi 56 | Réthimno | tel. 28 31* 05 29 20 | www.happywalker.nl/pages/ home_e.php)*. Mountaineering societies: *E.O.P. Chanioú (Odós Tzanakáki 90 | tel. 28 21 02 46 47)*; *P.O.H. Iraklíou (Mon–Fri 8.30–10.30am | Odós Dikeossíni 53 | tel. 28 10 22 76 09 | www.climbincrete.com)*; *E.O.P. Réthimno (Odós Moátsaou | in the ELTA building| tel. 28 31 02 27 10)*

HORSE RIDING

Riding stables for experienced riders are the INSIDER TIP *Horsefarm Melanoúri* in Pitsídia *(tel. 28 92 04 50 40 | www.melanouri.com/index_en.html)* and the *Odysseia Stables* in Avdoú en route to the Lassíthi Plateau *(tel. 28 97 05 10 80, mobile 69 42 83 60 83 | www.horseriding.gr)*.

MOUNTAIN BIKING

Crete is an ideal destination for mountain bikers. There are lots of good biking centres that offer a range of tour packages for all levels of difficulty. Those who prefer to take it easy can take a support van up to the starting point and then cycle downhill while ambitious bikers can challenge themselves cycling between mountain peaks.

Organisers offer day trips and weekend packages. Day tours cost between 40 and 60 euros, children pay approx. 25–40 euros. Some agencies only provide bicycles, like *Adventurebikes* in Georgioúpoli *(on the road heading for the motorway to Chaniá | tel. 28 25 06 18 30)*; *Hellas Bike* in Agía Marína in Chaniá *(main road opposite the Bank of Cyprus | tel. 28 21 06 08 58 | www.hellasbike.net)*; *Olympic Bike* on the coast road east of Réthimno *(Adelianós Kámbos 32 | tel. 28 31 07 27 83 | www.olympicbike.com)* and *Anso Travel* in Plakiás on the south coast *(tel. 28 32 03 17 12 | www.ansotravel.com)*. Prices depend on the type of bike and tour and cost between 13–22 euros a day or approx. 80–115 euros per week.

Motorbike tours are organised between May and October in the west *(Crete Unlimited | Michael Dirksen | Pigí/Réthimno | tel. 26 31 07 12 87 | www.excursions.creta-online.com)*.

SAILING

With an experienced skipper on board you can go sailing on a private yacht from Ágios Nikólaos to the islands of Spinalónga or Móchlos *(Pélagos Diving Centre | Minos Beach Hotel | tel. 28 41 02 43 76 | www.sailcrete.com)*. From Ierápetra you can sail to the island of Chrisí *(Nautilos | Odós Markopoúlou 1 | tel. 69 72 89 42 79 | www.nautiloscruises.gr)*. You are welcome to lend a hand but it is not necessary. Multiple day trips with different destinations can also be arranged.

WATER SPORTS

Almost all the popular beaches offer water sports options, from water skiing to jet skiing and paragliding. Paddle boats and canoes can also be hired in front of the larger hotels and surfboards are available on many of the beaches. Good surf schools can be found at the larger centres as well as by most of the Grecotels or the *Freak Station* on *Kourménos beach* in Palékastro, who also specialise in kite surfing *(tel. 28 43 06 11 16 and 69 79 25 38 61 | in the winter 0043 67 64 22 00 41 | www.freak-surf.com)*.

WELLNESS & YOGA

Many luxury hotels have spas that are also open to non-residents. ● Magical earth forces may be felt by yoga and t'ai chi practitioners and people attending meditational courses on the southern coast. More information *www.yogaplus. co.uk*.

Impressive views: hiking the Samariá Gorge

TRAVEL WITH KIDS

The most Cretans are very fond of children but this does not mean that the Cretans create special places for children. Playgrounds are not well designed and there are seldom special menus for children in the restaurants. However, children happily participate in adult life here even well after midnight.

There are also attractions where children can have lots of fun and there are many exhibits in the museums that children will find interesting if they are well prepared for them. If parents present the ruins of a building as a play house, it can keep the children busy for an hour or so and they will only start looking for their parents when the food in their fantasy kitchen has been cooked and the table has been laid with their fantasy dishes of grass and herbs.

CHANIÁ

TAKE A CARRIAGE THROUGH THE TOWN (135 E3) (*Ø D2*)

In the harbour at Chaniá there are always carriages waiting for customers. After negotiating a price you can drive around for half an hour in a horse-drawn carriage along the harbour and through the old town. *Platía Syntriváni exit | recommended price about 20 euros for 30 minutes.*

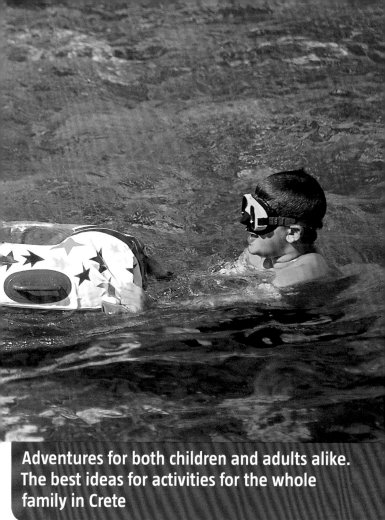

Adventures for both children and adults alike. The best ideas for activities for the whole family in Crete

VENETIAN MODEL
(135 E3) (*D2*)

Children do not always have a lot to do at archaeological ruins. But once they have seen the model of the Venetian arsenal in the Nautical Museum in Chaniá they might look at other ruins differently and be able to imagine the galleys and ships docks coming to life in the empty ruins. *Daily 9am–4pm, in the winter 10am–* *2pm | entrance 3 euros, children (6–17 years) 2 euros | Aktí Kunduriót | Chaniá*

GIANT SLIDE
(135 E3) (*C2*)

The *Limnoúpolis* water park in the west of Crete lies between the green hills of Varípetro, approx. 7 km (4¼ mi) outside of Chaniá. Here they have a giant slide and different swimming pools and playgrounds for every shape and size. *End May–Oct daily 10am–6pm | entrance until 3 pm 20 euros, children (6–12 years) 15 euros, from 3 pm 12 euros | buses from Platía 1866 in Chaniá | www.limnoupolis.gr*

RÉTHIMNO

BE A PIRATE
(137 D–E3) (*𝄐 F3*)

In the idyllic harbour of Réthimno, the *Captain Hook* comes in to anchor in the morning and evening. It looks like a real pirate ship and makes daily trips to *Maráthi* and *Balí*. Children (and pirates) with eye patches are welcome to come

Cretans are very fond of children

on board and might even receive a discount. *Info at the ship | ticket approx. 32 euros, children (6–12 years) 15 euros*

TAKE A MINI TRAIN
In many Cretan holiday destinations a small train, a ● *trenáki*, travels around between resorts. It runs on rubber wheels day and night through Réthimno (137 D–E3) (*𝄐 F3*) or from the hotels at Georgioúpoli (136 C3) (*𝄐 E3*) to Kournás and the village square. You can take a trip on the train or just use it as a means of transport. Either way, you will certainly enjoy the fresh air. On longer trips they also have tour guides who explain the points of interest along the way.

IRÁKLIO

ADVENTURE HOLIDAY
For families with children from about 12 years of age the club *Cretan Adventures* offers weekly programmes. The programme includes cave expeditions, rock climbing, sea kayaking, mountain biking, hikes and swimming. Airport transfers, accommodation and half-board is included in the price. *Cretan Adventures | Odós Evans 10 | Iráklio | tel. 28 10 33 27 72 | www.cretanadventures.gr).*

HORSE CARTS, PICNICS & PONIES
(139 E2) (*𝄐 K4*)

Grigórios is passionate horse lover. From his stables *Finíkia* south of Iráklio he offers three and a half hour tours on horse cart through Crete's green landscape, followed by a picnic on his own land. Children can also ride on ponies on the grounds of his second stable opposite the Star Water Park east of Liménas Chersónisou and at night under floodlights on request. *Finíkia Horse Riding Tours | pony rides approx. 8 euros/10 minutes horse cart tour including picnic approx. 60 euros, children from 14 years 30 euros | tel. 28 97 02 35 55, mobile 69 45 92 41 12*

DONKEY RIDES
(140 C3) (*M4*)

Manólis and his Swedish wife Karin have created a small paradise on INSIDER TIP *Kríti Farm*, where families can not only enjoy a 45 minute ride on a donkey or a 30 minute ride on a cart, but can also have a meal in the rustic, child-friendly surroundings. A small petting zoo is also available. *Ride 12 euros, cart tours 8 euros | beneath Chersónisos street on the Lassíthi Plateau just behind Potamiés | tel. 28 97 05 15 46*

WATER PARKS

As there is not much of a beach in Liménas Chersónisou, the two water parks are very popular. The *Star Beach Water Park* (140 C2) (*M3*) east of Liménas with its loud music is more focused on the youth and disco lovers *(daily 9am–7pm | admission free | on the coastal road at the eastern edge of Liménas Chersónisou)*. The *Acqua Plus* (140 B2) (*M4*) is a better option for families. Here you will find giant slides and lots of space to play. The park has transfer buses from Iráklio and other swimming locations. Information available at any hotel. *(Daily 10am–6pm | entrance before 2pm 20 euros, children (5–11 years) 12 euros, after 2pm 8 euros | 5 km (3 mi) inland on the road to Kastélli | www.acquaplus.gr).*

Lots of riding fun at the stables near Iráklio

IERÁPETRA

INSIDER TIP **PLAY ROBINSON CRUSOE**
(142 A6) (*O7*)

Excursion boats to the uninhabited island of Chrisí leave from Ierápetra daily. If you arrange it with the captain you can even have an adventure and stay overnight and camp on the beach. In the summer you don't even need a tent. You can take provisions with you but there are also two tavernas on the island. Take a torch along.

SITÍA

WALK THROUGH THE 'VALLEY OF THE DEAD' (143 E–F 3–4) (*R5*)

An easy two hour walk takes you from Zákros down to the beach at Káto Zákros. The caves can be a bit eerie and the huge oleander bushes create a fairytale forest and it is fun for children to cross streams on stepping stones. The reward at the end is fantastic – a refreshing swim.

FESTIVALS & EVENTS

The Cretans like to celebrate and a lot of the occasions for celebration are the various patron saint days. These village festivals usually start on the eve of the actual feast day with lots of music and dancing. On the day of the festival itself there is usually just a church service. Shrove Monday, Good Friday, Easter and Pentecost in the Greek Orthodox Church are celebrated according to the Julian calendar and rarely fall on our holy days.

During the summer, there are many music and cultural festivals in the villages. These festivals are held mainly for the locals and are usually advertised via posters in Greek. The programmes are unfortunately only published just before the event. Sometimes you can find the programme on the internet a few days in advance on *www.cultureguide.gr*.

PUBLIC HOLIDAYS

1 January New Year; **6 January** Epiphany; **25 March** Independence; **Shrove Monday** (27 Feb. 2012, 18 March 2013, 3 March 2014); **Good Friday** (13 April 2012, 3 May 2013, 18 April 2014); **Easter** (15/16 April 2012, 5/6 Mai 2013, 20/21 April 2014); May Day **1 May**; **Pentecost** (3/4 June 2012, 23/24 June 2013, 9/10 June 2014); **15 August** Assumption Day; **28 October** National day; **25/26 December** Christmas

FESTIVALS & EVENTS

CARNIVAL SUNDAY
▶ *Large carnival procession* through the main roads of Réthimno with thousands dressed in costumes, lots of themed floats and loud samba music with Greek lyrics

25 MARCH
▶ *Independence day* schoolchildren often wear costumes for the parades

EASTER FRIDAY
▶ *Processions* in all the towns and villages (from about 9pm)

EASTER SATURDAY
▶ *Easter fairs* from 11pm with fireworks shortly after midnight

Church fairs and processions: Crete's holiday calendar is defined by the Greek Orthodox Church's festivals

SUNDAY AFTER EASTER
▶ *Church service in the cave at Mílatos* followed by free entertainment and refreshments for guests at the square

21 MAY
▶ *Parish fair* with music and dancing in *Gra Ligiá* at Ierápetra

JULY–SEPTEMBER
▶ INSIDER TIP ▶ *Renaissance festival in Réthimno:* The festival with the most extensive programme in Crete, offering performances, theatre pieces and concerts which pay homage to the Renaissance period. The preferred place for events is the amphitheatre in the Fortézza of Réthimno (starting July–mid Sept). *www.rethymnon.gr*
▶ *Cultural festival* in Iráklio with many events at different places in the city. *www.heraklion-city.gr*

AUGUST
▶ *Community festival in Anógia* with *lýra* competitions, singing and Cretan dancing (starting August)
▶ *Parish festivals* with lots of music and dancing as well as festivals in town squares in almost all the Cretan villages (14/15 Aug)
▶ *Potato festival* in Tzermiádo on the Lassíthi Plateau with music, dancing, a market and free potato tasting (weekends after the 15th of Aug)
▶ *Culture festival* in Krítsa in Ágios Nikólaos with theatre, dancing and folklore evenings (15–30 Aug)
▶ *Ágios Títos:* procession with St Titus's skull relic through Iráklio (25 Aug)

OCTOBER
▶ *Parish festival at the Guvernétu Monastery* in Chaniá with a procession from the monastery to the cave for a festival service (7 Oct)

LINKS, BLOGS, APPS & MORE

LINKS

▶ www.infocrete.com links to the top 100 websites about Crete

▶ wwww.explorecrete.com comprehensive website with full of tourist information, with local news, maps and climate charts

▶ www.bbc.co.uk/languages/greek for some essential Greek phrases and an introduction to basic Greek as well as links to other free courses, a slide show and video

▶ www.crete-kreta-kriti.com links every website in Crete! Absolutely everything you need to know from A to Z

▶ www.crete.gr a website with information on the island's history, climate and environmental issues as well as what to do and where to eat

BLOGS & FORUMS

▶ www.livingincrete-carolina.blogspot.com blog about the 'ups and downs' of the expat life in Crete by Carol Palioudakis the author of the book *Living in Crete: A Guide to Living, Working, Retiring & Buying Property in Crete*

▶ www.cretegazette.com an online newspaper for Crete's English community with local news and articles about everyday events in Crete

▶ www.completely-crete.com was set up by two UK expats in order to share their insider knowledge about Crete. The site is very comprehensive with lots of listings for restaurants, accommodation as well as history, culture and various services

Regardless of whether you are still preparing your trip or already in Crete: these addresses will provide you with more information, videos and networks to make your holiday even more enjoyable

VIDEOS

▶ www.explorecrete.com/videos/crete-videos.html a wide selection of good quality videos showcasing Cretan villages, beaches, archaeological sites as well as cultural videos about music, dance and Crete's traditions

APPS

▶ Save Minotaur! You have to make your way through the labyrinth to save the Minotaur. The game has different levels of difficulty to suit all ages

▶ Crete Street Map Load this onto your iPhone and have instant access to the island's city streets even when you have no internet access

▶ Myths of Crete & Pre-Hellenic For those interested in the history and myths of Crete this app forms part of the e-book by Donald A Mackenzie. The app is for smartphones iPhones

NETWORK

▶ twitter.com/#!/cretegreece twitter page that celebrates the best of Crete with regular news and updates

▶ www.airbnb.com/greece is the popular site for travellers who prefer to stay in private accommodation offered by locals. A search under Crete pulls ups the full spectrum from rooms in private homes through to luxury villas and boutique hotels. The site is constantly updated with new listings and user reviews.

▶ www.facebook.com/pages/Crete/27360964589 Facebook page for Crete that has lots of private photos and comments from the international community

TRAVEL TIPS

ARRIVAL

There are daily flights to Crete via Olympic Air *(www.olympicair.com)*, Athens Airways *(www.athensairways.com)* and Aegean Airlines *(www.aegeanair.com)* from Athens. Between Easter and October there are also many direct charter and package flights that go directly to Iráklio and Chaniá but these can sometimes be more expensive than normal airline flights. Flights from London to Iráklio take about 3 and a half hours and from Athens about 40 minutes. At both airports there are taxis for further transport. At Iráklio there are also reasonably priced buses that go to the nearby city centre. From Chaniá's airport there are only a few buses that leave for the city centre. Crete's third biggest airport in Sitía sees weekly flights from Olympic Air and Aegean Airlines from Athens. Taxis are also available at the airport.

RESPONSIBLE TRAVEL

It doesn't take a lot to be environmentally friendly whilst travelling. Don't just think about your carbon footprint whilst flying to and from your holiday destination but also about how you can protect nature and culture abroad. As a tourist it is especially important to respect nature, look out for local products, cycle instead of driving, save water and much more. If you would like to find out more about eco-tourism please visit: *www.ecotourism.org*

Ferries travel daily from Piraeus in Athens to Chaniá, Iráklio and Réthimno (6–12 hours) and weekly to Ágios Nikólaos and Sitía. Compare prices at *www.gtp.gr, www.greekferries.gr, www.minoan.gr, www.superfast.com* or contact a travel agent.

BUS

There are regular public buses to almost every town in Crete and travelling by bus is recommended. The blue buses only travel within municipal districts. Long distance buses (often green) travel between Iráklio, Ágios Nikólaos, Chaniá, Ierápetra, Sitía and Réthimno. Tickets are bought in the cities and should be shown on the bus. Tickets for city buses can be bought at kiosks, hotel receptions and shops.
Timetables for western Crete can be found on: *www.bus-service-crete-ktel.com,* and for eastern Crete on: *www.ktel-heraklio-lassithi.gr*

CAMPING

Camping anywhere else but in a camp site is prohibited in Crete but is often done on isolated beaches. There are a total of 16 camping sites on the island that are open between April and October.

CAR HIRE

Bicycles, mopeds, motor scooters, motorbikes, 4x4s and cars can be rented in most of the holiday resorts on Crete. To rent a car you must have had your driver's license for more than a year and be over 21. A small car will cost about 30 euros per day including miles driven, full comprehensive cover and tax. The maximum speed in country areas is 50 km/h and on national roads 90 km/h. It is compulsory to wear seatbelts in the front seats Maximum blood alcohol level is 0.5; 0.2 for motorbike riders. Cretans are notorious for cutting curves, so always keep to the right of the road. Also get used to honking at blind corners! During autumn, the roads are especially wet and slippery and care should be taken.

Breakdown assistance can be obtained from the automobile club *ELPA*, country wide *tel. 1 04 00*

CONSULATES & EMBASSIES

BRITISH EMBASSY
1 Ploutarhou Str. | 10675 Athens | tel. 210 72 36 21 19 | ukingreece.fco.gov.uk

BRITISH CONSULATE
Candia Tower | 17 Thalita Street | Ag. Dimitrios Sq. | Iráklio | tel. 28 10 22 40 12 | crete@fco.gov.uk

CANADIAN EMBASSY
4 Ioannou Ghennadiou Street | 11521 Athens, Greece | tel. 210 7 27 34 00 | www. canadainternational.gc.ca/greece-grece

US EMBASSY
91 Vasilissis Sophias Avenue | Athens | tel. 210 7 21 29 51 | AthensAmEmb@state.gov | athens.usembassy.gov

CUSTOMS

EU citizens can import and export goods for their personal use tax-free (800 cigarettes, 1 kg tobacco, 90 L of wine, 10 L of

BUDGETING

Boat tour	28 euros *all day, without transfer*
Coffee	1.20 to 2.80 euros *for an espresso*
Gyros	3 euros *for gyros and a pita bread*
Wine	2 to 5 euros *for a glass*
Petrol	1.70 euros *for a litre Super*
Deckchair	7 to 10 euros *per day together with umbrella*

spirits over 22 %). Visitors from other countries must observe the following limits, except for items for personal use. Duty free are: max. 50 g perfume, 200 cigarettes, 50 cigars, 250 g tobacco, 1 L of spirits (over 22 % vol.), 2 L of spirits (under 22 % vol.), 2 L of any wine. Gifts to the value of up to 175 euros may be brought into Greece.

DRINKING WATER

It is safe to drink the chlorinated tap water everywhere except Iráklio. Still mineral water *(metallikó neró)* is also available in restaurants and cafés and is usually the same price as in the supermarkets.

EARTHQUAKES

Light earthquakes do occur and should you experience an earthquake you should

Ottoman heritage – wooden balconies in the old town

Entry to all archaeological sites and state museums is free for children and youths, as well as students from EU member states who have appropriate ID. Senior citizens from EU countries, 65 years and older get a 30 per cent discount. From November to March, entrance is free on Sundays for all visitors. Other free entrance days are the first Sunday in April, May and October, the 6th of March, the last weekend in September, all international observances like International Remembrance Day in April, International Museum Day in May, World Environment Day in June and World Tourism Day in September.

There is no entrance fee for visiting churches and monasteries but donations are always welcome. The most discreet way to do this is to buy candles and light them in front of an icon with a prayer of intercession.

HEALTH

Well-trained doctors guarantee basic medical care throughout Crete, however there is often a lack of technical equipment. If you are seriously ill, it is advisable to return home and this will be covered by your travel insurance. Emergency treatment in hospitals is free of charge and you can be treated for free by doctors if you present the European Health Insurance Card issued by your own insurance company. However, in practice this is complicated and doctors do so reluctantly and it is better to pay cash, get a receipt and then present your bills to the insurance company for a refund.

Most towns and villages have chemists that are are well-stocked but they may not always have British medication. In Greece, many branded medicines which are only available if you have a prescription in other

take cover underneath a table or a bed. As soon as the quake is over you should go outside (but do not use the lifts) and then stay clear of walls and flower pots that might topple over. Once outside follow the lead of the locals.

ELECTRICITY

Crete has the same 220 volt as most continental European countries. You will need an adapter if you want to use a UK plug.

EMERGENCY SERVICES

112 for all the emergency services: police, fire brigade and ambulance. The number is toll free and English is also spoken.

countries, can be purchased without one and are cheaper than at home. These include painkillers and remedies for heartburn and herpes. You are only able to import small quantities to protect the financial interests of the pharmaceutical industry.

IMMIGRATION

A valid passport is required for entry into Greece. Children under 12 years need their own passport.

INFORMATION

The Hellenic Ministry of Culture and Tourism website has explanations, photos and information on opening times and entrance prices of all excavations and many museums: *www.culture.gr*

GREEK NATIONAL TOURISM ORGANISATION (UK)
4 Conduit Street | London, W1S 2DJ | tel. 020 7495 9300 | www.visitgreece.gr

GREEK NATIONAL TOURISM ORGANISATION (US)
305 East 47th Street | New York 10017 | tel. 212 4 21 57 77 | www.greektourism.com

LANGUAGE

The Greeks are very proud of their language characters which are unique to Greece. More place names are being written in Roman letters but it is still helpful to have some knowledge of the Greek alphabet. However there is no uniform transliteration so the same name can have four different versions.

Sometimes the accents on addresses, hotel names and restaurant names are missing when written. The locals seldom call places by their proper names. Cretans name hotels and tavernas according to the owner and when giving addresses would rather name important points rather than a street name. The names of hotels and tavernas are not written as they are pronounced, but rather the way that they are written on signs.

MONEY & CREDIT CARDS

The national currency is the euro. You can withdraw money from many cash machines with your credit or debit card. Banks and post offices cash traveller's cheques. Credit cards (especially Visa and MasterCard) are accepted by many hotels and restaurants but only by a few petrol stations, tavernas and shops. Bank open-

CURRENCY CONVERTER

£	€	€	£
1	1.20	1	0.85
3	3.60	3	2.55
5	6	5	4.25
13	15.60	13	11
40	48	40	34
75	90	75	64
120	144	120	100
250	300	250	210
500	600	500	425

$	€	€	$
1	0.75	1	1.30
3	2.30	3	3.90
5	3.80	5	6.50
13	10	13	17
40	30	40	50
75	55	75	97
120	90	120	155
250	185	250	325
500	370	500	650

For current exchange rates see www.xe.com

ing hours are *Mon–Thu 8am–2pm, Fri 8am–1.30pm*.

NEWSPAPERS

English magazines and newspapers are available at most holiday resorts on the island. The weekly English *Athens News* is also published.

NUDIST BEACHES

Nude bathing is prohibited, but is practised on many isolated beaches. The only official nudist beach in Crete, lies west of west of Chóra Sfakíon at the only nudist hotel in Greece, the Hotel Vritomártis. Topless sunbathing is accepted everywhere.

ORGANISED TOURS

All the holiday resorts and hotels offer organised excursions by bus or boat. Bus tours are done with local and licensed guides. Sometimes hikes and boat trips with transfer from the hotel to harbour and back are on the programme.

PHONE & MOBILE PHONE

With the exception of some emergency numbers, all Greek telephone numbers have ten digits. There is no area dialling code. Greek mobile phone numbers always begin with '6'. Telephone booths with card telephones are very common in the cities, villages and on country roads. They are mainly operated by the telephone company OTE/COSMOTE which has offices in most cities. Telephone cards can be bought at kiosks and supermarkets.

Mobile phones are popular in Greece and reception is also very good. When buying a Greek SIM card to obtain a Greek telephone number, you always will have to present identification. SIM cards can be brought from about 5 euros and remain valid for a year after last use. Mobile phone service providers are Cosmote, Vodafone and Wind.

The dialling code for Greece is *0030* followed by the full ten digit telephone number. International dialling codes: United Kingdom *0044*, Australia *0061*, Canada *001*, Ireland *00353*, USA *001* followed by the area code without the zero.

POST

There are post offices in all the cities and larger villages. Business hours are: Mon–Fri 7am–3pm, in the tourism centres sometimes later in the afternoon as well as Saturday mornings.

TAXI

Taxis can be found everywhere and are relatively cheap. In the country they are called *agoraíon* and have no taxi meters – the price is calculated according to the distance.

TIME ZONE

Greece is two hours ahead of Greenwich Mean Time, seven hours ahead of US Eastern Time and seven hours behind Australian Eastern Time.

TIPPING

Tips are only expected in large tourist areas and small tips are seen as an insult. Tips are left on the table when leaving.

TOILETS

Apart from those in hotels, Crete's toilets can come as a surprise. They can be perfectly acceptable but at other times should only be used in emergencies. Be aware that even in the good hotels you are not allowed to flush the used toilet paper down the drain, but have to throw it in the bin provided. The reason for this is that the paper clogs up the island's narrow sewers and soakaways.

WEATHER & CLIMATE

Crete is not a winter holiday destination. Between November and March it can rain and be quite cool. The best holiday months are from April to October. Swimming is best between May and November. May is the most beautiful time to travel in Crete, it is very green and there are flowers are in bloom everywhere. It hardly rains from June to September and temperatures can reach 40° C (104° F) and the average temperatures for July and August is 30 degrees (86 Fahrenheit) by day and 20 degrees (68 Fahrenheit) at night. There are also often strong winds on Crete that can even bring the ferries to a standstill.

YOUTH HOSTELS

In Crete there are many simple accommodation units that call themselves 'youth hostels' but none of them are members of the international Youth Hostel Society. They are mostly privately owned. The only 'youth hostel' worth recommending is the one in Plakiás.

WEATHER IN IRÁKLIO

	Jan	Feb	March	April	May	June	July	Aug	Sept	Oct	Nov	Dec
Daytime temperatures in °C/°F	16/61	16/61	1763	20/68	24/75	28/82	29/84	29/84	27/81	24/75	21/70	17/63
Nighttime temperatures in °C/°F	9/48	9/48	10/50	12/54	15/59	19/66	21/70	22/72	19/66	16/61	14/57	11/52
Sunshine hours/day	3	5	6	8	10	12	13	12	10	6	6	4
Precipitation days/month	12	7	8	4	2	1	0	0	2	6	6	10
Water temperatures in °C/°F	16/61	15/59	16/61	16/61	19/66	22/72	24/75	25/77	24/75	23/73	20/68	17/63

USEFUL PHRASES GREEK

PRONUNCIATION

We have provided a simple pronunciation aid for the Greek words
(see middle column). Note the following:

'   the following syllable is emphasised
ð   in Greek (shown as "dh" in middle column) is like "th" in "there"
θ   in Greek (shown as "th" in middle column) is like "th" in "think"
Χ   in Greek (shown as "ch" in middle column) is like a rough "h" or
    "ch" in Scottish "loch"

A	α	a		H	η	i		N	ν	n
B	β	v		Θ	θ	th		Ξ	ξ	ks, x
Γ	γ	g, y		I	ι	i, y		O	ο	o
Δ	δ	th		K	κ	k		Π	π	p
E	ε	e		Λ	λ	l		P	ρ	r
Z	ζ	z		M	μ	m		Σ	σ, ς	s, ss

T	τ	t
Y	υ	i, y
Φ	φ	f
X	χ	ch
Ψ	ψ	ps
Ω	ώ	o

IN BRIEF

Yes/No/Maybe	ne/'ochi/'issos	Ναι/ Όχι/Ισως
Please/Thank you	paraka'lo/efcharis'to	Παρακαλώ/Ευχαριστώ
Sorry	sig'nomi	Συγνώμη
Excuse me	me sig'chorite	Με συγχωρείτε
May I ...?	epi'treppete ...?	Επιτρέπεται …?
Pardon?	o'riste?	Ορίστε?
I would like to .../	'thelo .../	Θέλω …/
have you got ...?	'echete ...?	Έχετε …?
How much is ...?	'posso 'kani ...?	Πόσο κάνει …?
I (don't) like this	Af'to (dhen) mu a'ressi	Αυτό (δεν) μου αρέσει
good/bad	ka'llo/kak'ko	καλό/κακό
too much/much/little	'para pol'li/pol'li/ligo	πάρα πολύ/πολύ/λίγο
everything/nothing	ólla/'tipottal	όλα/τίποτα
Help!/Attention!/	vo'ithia!/prosso'chi!/	Βοήθεια!/Προσοχή!/
Caution!	prosso'chi!	Προσοχή!
ambulance	astheno'forro	Ασθενοφόρο
police/	astino'mia/	Αστυνομία/
fire brigade	pirosvesti'ki	Πυροσβεστική
ban/	apa'gorefsi/	Απαγόρευση/
forbidden	apago'revete	απαγορεύεται
danger/dangerous	'kindinoss/epi'kindinoss	Κίνδυνος/επικίνδυνος

Milás elliniká?

"Do you speak Greek?" This guide will help you to say the basic words and phrases in Greek.

GREETINGS, FAREWELL

Good morning!/after-	kalli'mera/kalli'mera!/	Καλημέρα/Καλημέρα!/
noon!/evening!/night!	kalli'spera!/kalli'nichta!	Καλησπέρα!/Καληνύχτα!
Hello!/	'ya (su/sass)!/a'dio!/	Γεία (σου/σας)!/αντίο!/
goodbye!	ya (su/sass)!	Γεία (σου/σας)!
Bye!	me 'lene ...	Με λένε ...
My name is ...	poss sass 'lene?	Πως σας λένε;

DATE & TIME

Monday/Tuesday	dhef'tera/'triti	Δευτέρα/Τρίτη
Wednesday/Thursday	tet'tarti/'pempti	Τετάρτη/Πέμπτη
Friday/Saturday	paraske'vi/'savatto	Παρασκευή/Σάββατο
Sunday/weekday	kiria'ki/er'gassimi	Κυριακή/Εργάσιμη
today/tomorrow/yesterday	'simera/'avrio/chtess	Σήμερα/Αύριο/Χτες
What time is it?	ti 'ora 'ine?	Τι ώρα είναι;

TRAVEL

open/closed	annik'ta/klis'to	Ανοικτό/Κλειστό
entrance/	'issodhos/	Είσοδος/
driveway	'issodhos ochi'matonn	Είσοδος οχημάτων
exit/exit	'eksodhos/	Έξοδος/
	'Eksodos ochi'matonn	Έξοδος οχημάτων
departure/	anna'chorissi/	Αναχώρηση/
departure/arrival	anna'chorissi/'afiksi	Αναχώρηση/Άφιξη
toilets/restrooms / ladies/	tual'lettes/gine'konn/	Τουαλέτες/Γυναικών/
gentlemen	an'dronn	Ανδρών
(no) drinking water	'possimo ne'ro	Πόσιμο νερό
Where is ...?/Where are ...?	pu 'ine ...?/pu 'ine ...?	Πού είναι/Πού είναι ...;
bus/taxi	leofo'rio/tak'si	Λεωφορείο/Ταξί
street map/	'chartis tis 'pollis/	Χάρτης της πόλης/
map	'chartis	Χάρτης
harbour	li'mani	Λιμάνι
airport	a-ero'drommio	Αεροδρόμιο
schedule/ticket	drommo'logio/issi'tirio	Δρομολόγιο/Εισιτήριο
I would like to rent ...	'thelo na nik'yasso ...	Θέλω να νοικιάσω ...
a car/a bicycle/	'enna afto'kinito/'enna	ένα αυτοκίνητο/ένα
a boat	po'dhilato/'mia 'varka	ποδήλατο/μία βάρκα
petrol/gas station	venzi'nadiko	Βενζινάδικο
petrol/gas / diesel	ven'zini/'diesel	Βενζίνη/Ντίζελ

FOOD & DRINK

Could you please book a table for tonight for four?	Klis'te mass parakal'lo 'enna tra'pezi ya a'popse ya 'tessera 'atoma	Κλείστε μας παρακαλώ ένα τραπέζι γιά απόψε γιά τέσσερα άτομα
The menu, please	tonn ka'taloggo parakal'lo	Τον κατάλογο παρακαλώ
Could I please have ...?	tha 'ithella na 'echo ...?	Θα ήθελα να έχω ...?
with/without ice/ sparkling	me/cho'ris 'pago/ anthrakik'ko	με/χωρίς πάγο/ ανθρακικό
vegetarian/allergy	chorto'fagos/allerg'ia	Χορτοφάγος/Αλλεργία
May I have the bill, please?	'thel'lo na pli'rosso parakal'lo	Θέλω να πληρώσω παρακαλώ

SHOPPING

Where can I find...?	pu tha vro ...?	Που θα βρω ...?
pharmacy/ chemist	farma'kio/ ka'tastima	Φαρμακείο/Κατάστημα καλλυντικών
bakery/market	'furnos/ago'ra	Φούρνος/Αγορά
grocery	pandopo'lio	Παντοπωλείο
kiosk	pe'riptero	Περίπτερο
expensive/cheap/price	akri'vos/fti'nos/ti'mi	ακριβός/φτηνός/Τιμή
more/less	pio/li'gotere	πιό/λιγότερο

ACCOMMODATION

I have booked a room	'kratissa 'enna do'matio	Κράτησα ένα δωμάτιο
Do you have any ... left?	'echete a'komma ...	Έχετε ακόμα ...
single room	mon'noklino	Μονόκλινο
double room	'diklino	Δίκλινο
key	kli'dhi	Κλειδί
room card	ilektronni'ko kli'dhi	Ηλεκτρονικό κλειδί

HEALTH

doctor/dentist/ paediatrician	ya'tros/odhondoya'tros/ pe'dhiatros	Ιατρός/Οδοντογιατρός/ Παιδίατρος
hospital/ emergency clinic	nossoko'mio/ yatri'ko 'kentro	Νοσοκομείο/ Ιατρικό κέντρο
fever/pain	piret'tos/'ponnos	Πυρετός/Πόνος
diarrhoea/nausea	dhi'arria/ana'gula	Διάρροια/Αναγούλα
sunburn	ilia'ko 'engavma	Ηλιακό έγκαυμα
inflamed/ injured	molli'menno/ pligo'menno	μολυμένο /πληγωμένο
pain reliever/tablet	paf'siponna/'chapi	Παυσίπονο/Χάπι

POST, TELECOMMUNICATIONS & MEDIA

stamp/letter	gramma'tossimo/'gramma	Γραμματόσημο/Γράμμα
postcard	kartpos'tall	Καρτ-ποστάλ
I need a landline phone card	kri'azomme 'mia tile'karta ya dhi'mossio tilefoni'ko 'thalamo	Χρειάζομαι μία τηλεκάρτα για δημόσιο τηλεφωνικό θάλαμο
I'm looking for a prepaid card for my mobile	tha 'ithella 'mia 'karta ya to kinni'to mu	Θα ήθελα μία κάρτα για το κινητό μου
Where can I find internet access?	pu bor'ro na vro 'prosvassi sto índernett?	Που μπορώ να βρω πρόσβαση στο ίντερνετ;
socket/adapter/charger	'briza/an'dapporras/fortis'tis	πρίζα/αντάπτορας/φορτιστής
computer/battery/rechargeable battery	ippologis'tis/batta'ria/eppanaforti'zomenni batta'ria	Υπολογιστής/μπαταρία/επαναφορτιζόμενη μπαταρία
internet connection/wifi	'sindhessi se as'sirmato 'dhitio/vaifai	Σύνδεση σε ασύρματο δίκτυο/WiFi

LEISURE, SPORTS & BEACH

beach	para'lia	Παραλία
sunshade/lounger	om'brella/ksap'plostra	Ομπρέλα/Ξαπλώστρα

NUMBERS

0	mi'dhen	μηδέν
1	'enna	ένα
2	'dhio	δύο
3	'tria	τρία
4	'tessera	τέσσερα
5	'pende	πέντε
6	'eksi	έξι
7	ef'ta	εφτά
8	och'to	οχτώ
9	e'nea	εννέα
10	'dhekka	δέκα
11	'endhekka	ένδεκα
12	'dodhekka	δώδεκα
20	'ikossi	είκοσι
50	pen'inda	πενήντα
100	eka'to	εκατό
200	dhia'kossia	διακόσια
1000	'chilia	χίλια
10000	'dhekka chil'iades	δέκα χιλιάδες

NOTES

MARCO POLO TRAVEL GUIDES

MARCO ☉ POLO

With ROAD ATLAS & PULL-OUT MAP

LAKE GARDA

MONTE BALDO WITH MOUNTAIN BIKE
The cable car in Malcesine takes bikes too

"KISSES" IN SALÒ
The chocolate "baceni"

Travel with
Insider Tips

MARCO ☉ POLO

With STREET ATLAS & PULL-OUT MAP

NEW YORK

MEADOWS, WILD FLOWERS AND SKYSCRAPERS
Green is chic: the High Line in Chelsea

COCKTAIL ON CLOUD NINE
The rooftop bar at 230 Fifth Street

Travel with
Insider Tips

MARCO ☉ POLO

With ROAD ATLAS & PULL-OUT MAP

FRENCH RIVIERA
NICE, CANNES & MONACO

SPECTACULAR GRAND CANYON DU VERDON
Breath-taking scenery that takes some beating

SNIFFING THE AIR
The perfume manufacturers of Grasse

Travel with
Insider Tips

www.marco-polo.com

MARCO ☉ POLO

With ROAD ATLAS & PULL-OUT MAP

MALLORCA

AN FLAIR IN THE MEDITERRANEAN
Mallorca's most beautiful beach

THE "IN" CROWD MEET
Fonda in Deià

Travel with
Insider Tips

MARCO ☉ POLO

With STREET ATLAS & PULL-OUT MAP

BERLIN

A STUNNING ISLAND JUST FOR ART
Showcasing treasures from around the world

STAY COOL AT NIGHT
The club scene sets the trend

Travel with
Insider Tips

- PACKED WITH INSIDER TIPS
- BEST WALKS AND TOURS
- FULL-COLOUR PULL-OUT MAP
  AND STREET ATLAS

www.marco-polo.com

ROAD ATLAS

The green line ▬ indicates the Trips & tours (p. 102–107)
The blue line ▬ indicates the Perfect route (p. 30–31)

All tours are also marked on the pull-out map

Photo: Mátala bay

Exploring Crete

The map on the back cover shows how the area has been sub-divided

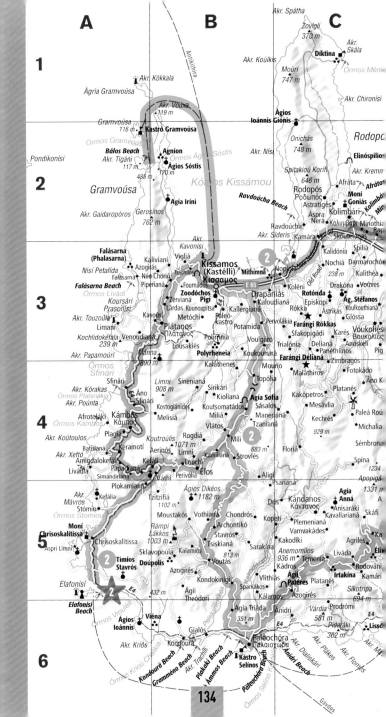

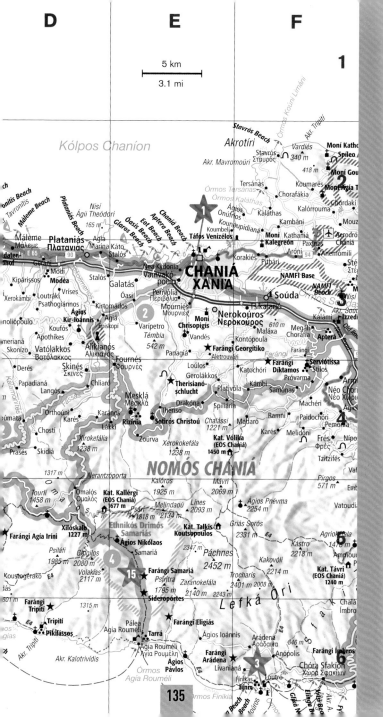

D
E
F

5 km
3.1 mi

Kólpos Chaníon

Akrotíri

Stavrós Beach

Akr. Mavromoúri

Vardiés
Stavrós
Σταυρός
340 m
418 m

Moní Katho
Spíleo

Moní Gou
Moní Agía T

Tersánas
Chorafákia
Koumarés
Chordakí

Órmos Tersanás
Órmos Kaláthas

Agios
Onoúfrios
Kounoupidianá
Kalathás
Kalórrouma
Kambáni
Mouz

Tsantouloú
Nisí
Ágii Theódori
165 m

Máleme
Μάλεμε

Plataniás
Πλατανιάς

Agía
Marina

Stalós

Chaniá Beach
Aptéra Beach
Eot Beach
Óasis Beach
Glaros Beach

Táfos Venizélos

Moni Kathaná
Kalegreón

Korakiés
Pithári
Aróni

Pachnís

Aerodró
Chaniá
Anemómili
Ste
Sté

Káto
Stalós

Néa Kydonía
Vamvakó
poúla

Máleme
Μάλεμε
Gerani
Kipárissos

Móði
Modéa

Stalós
CHANIÁ
XANIÁ

NAMFI Base

Soúda
NAMFI
Beach

Órmos Soúd
Izzedd

Xerokámbi
Loutráki
Psathógiannos
Vríses

Galatás

Óasis

Perivólia
Περιβόλια

Mourniés
Μουρνιές

Nerokoúros
Νερόκουρος

Tsikalariá
Kálami
Megáli
Chorafiá
Aptéra

610 m
Maláxa

nolioúpoulo
Kir-Ioánnis
Agía
Episkopí

Varipetro
Témbla
542 m

Vandés

Moní
Chrisopigís

Panagiá

★ **Farángi Georgítiko**
Aletrouvári

Farángi
Farángi

Ágios

★ **Farángi**
Díktamos

Katochóri
Loúlos
Gerolákkos

Serviótissa
Stílos

Néo Chor
Néo Χλωρ

Armí

Kontópoula

meriamá
Skonízo
Vatólakkos
Βατόλακκος

Derés

Alikianós
Αλικιανός

Skinés
ΣΚΙΝΕΣ

Fournés
Φουρνές

Papadianá
Langós

Chliaró

★ **Therisianó-**
schlucht

Plativóla

Kámbi
Samonás

Próvarma

Machéri
Paidochóri

Néo Chorí

Pemonía

Orthoúni
Karés

Mesklá
Μεσκλά

Karános
λάκκι

Rizínia

Theríso

Drakóna
Spiliaría

Sotíros Christoú

Chalássi
1221 m

Madaró

Ramni

Karés
Melidóni

Nípo
Φρές

Chostí

Xirokefália
1238 m

Zoúrva

Xerokokefála
1238 m

Kat. Vólika
(EOS Chaniá)
1450 m

Tzitzifés

Prasés
Skidiá

NOMÓS CHANIÁ

1317 m
Nerantzópora

Kallóros
Mávri
2069 m

Pírgos
571 m

Vat

Emb

Toúrli
1458 m

Omalós
Ωμαλός

Kat. Kallérgi
(EOS Chaniá)
1677 m

Psári
1818 m

Melindaoú
2134 m

Línes
2093 m

Agios Pnévma
2254 m

Vatoudiá

Farángi Agía Iríni

Xilóskalo
1227 m

Ethnikós Drimós
Samariás

Kat. Talkis
Koutsopoúlos

Griás Sorós
2331 m

E4

Kástro
2218 m

Agrioláka
1478 m

Ammoú

Psiláfi
1985 m

Gíngilos
2080 m

Agios Nikólaos
Samariá

2347 m

Páchnes
2452 m

Kakovóli

Trocharís
2214 m

Kat. Távri
(EOS Chaniá)
1240 m

Koustogerakó

Volakiás
2117 m

★ **Farángi Samariá**

Psilrítra
1795 m

Zaránokefála
2140 m 2243 m

2401 m 2008 m

Chalá
Ímbro

Sideropórtes

Lefká Óri

Farángi
Tripití

Tripití

1315 m

Pikíllasos

Pálea
Agía Rouméli

★ **Farángi Eligiás**

Ágios Ioánnis

E4

Tarrá

Agia Rouméli
Αγία Ρουμελη

Agios
Pávlos

Órmos
Agía Rouméli

Órmos Finika

Farángi
Arádena

Livanianá

Arádena
Αράδαινα

846 m

Anópolis

Farángi Ímbro

Chóra Sfakíon
Χώρα Σφακίων

Fínikas

Loutró

Fínix

Akr. Kalotrivídis

Akr. Tripití

135

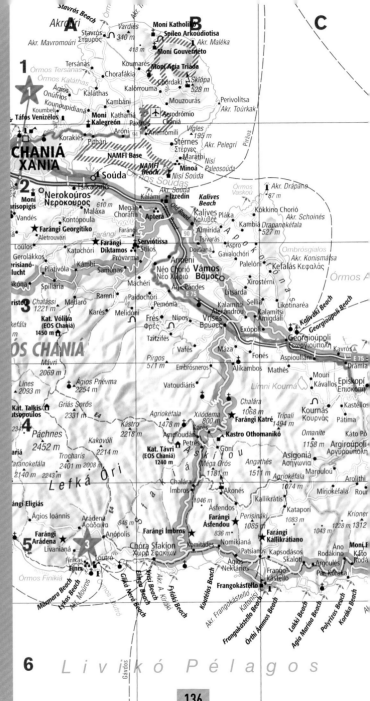

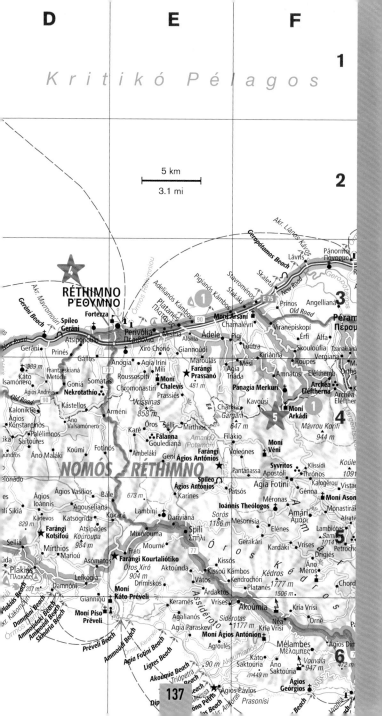

Kritikó Pélagos

5 km

3.1 mi

Akr. Liános Kavós

Geropótamos Beach

Pánormo
Πάνορμο

Lávris

Geropotamos

Akr. Mavromoúri
RÉTHIMNO
P'EΘYMNO

Geráni Beach
Spíleo
Geráni

Fortézza

Pigianós Kámbos

Adelianós Kámbos

Ormós Rethímnou

Platanés
Πλατανές

Stavroménos

Sfakáki

Pánormo

New Road

Skaléta

E 75

Prínos
Old Road

Angelliná

Péram
Πέραμ

Gerapótamos

3

New Road

Atsipópoulo

Perivólia
Περιβόλια

Misiriá

Chamalévri

Moní Arsáni

Viranepiskopí

Érfi
Álfa

Gállos

Xiró Chorió

Adele

Pigí

Loútra

Kiriánna

Skouloúfia
Vergianá

Geráni

Prínes

Giannoúdi

Maroulás

Mési

Amnátos

Eléftherna

Orthé

Anógia

Agía Iríni

Mili

Agía
Triáda

Panagía Merkúri

Archéa
Eléftherna

Archéa

Frantzeskianá
Metóchi

989 m

Káto
Isamónero

Ágios Andréas

Somatás

Roussospíti

Farángi
Prassanó

Kavoúsi

Moní
Arkádi

Eléftherna

Old Road

Nekrotathío

Chromonastíri

Moní
Chalévis

481 m

Prassiés

Charkía
Gargáni

Mávrou Korifí
944 m

Kástellos

Vríssinas
858 m

Kaloníkti

Ágios
Konstantínos

 Áno
Valsamónero

Karé

Óros
Sélli

Mírthios

647 m

Palélimnos

Saïtoúres

Koúmi

Fotinós

Fálanna
Goulediáná

Amánou
(Potamón)

Filáki

Moní
Véni

NOMÓS RÉTHIMNO

Ambelakí

Gení

Ágios Antónios

Voleónes

Pantánassa

Syvrítos
Apóstoli

Thrónos

Klissídi

Koúle
1091

Ágios Vasílios

673 m

Spíleo
Ágios Antónios

Génna

Kalogérou

Moní Asom

Vistag

Ágios
Ioánnis

Agouseliná

Patsós

Agía Fotiní

Méronas

Amári
Αμάρι

Monastirá

Afraté

Kánevos

Katsogrída

Koxaré

Lambíni

Dariviáná

Ioánnis Theológos

Samá
1014

Faràngi
Kotsifoú

Atsipádes
Koúroupa
904 m

Mixórouma

Sorós
1186 m

Mesonísia

Elénes

Kardáki

Lambiótes

Vríses

Petroch

Mirthíos

Marioú

Fráti

Mourné

Spíli
Σπήλι

Gerakári

Ásomatos

Óros Xiró
904 m

Faràngi Kourtaliótiko

Aktoúnda

Kissós

Óros

Áno
Méros

Drígiés

Kissoú Kámbos

Kédros
1777 m

Chord

Plakiás

Damnóni

Lefkógia

Moní
Káto Préveli

Giannioú

Drímiskos

Vátos

Kendrochóri

Platanés

1506 m

207 m

Keramés

Árdaktos

Vríses

Akoúmia

Kría Vrisi

Préveli Beach

Moní Píso
Préveli

Agía Paraskeví

Agalianós

Síderotas

Moní Ágios Antónios

Sideróta
1177 m

Kría Vrisi

Órne

Néa

Mélambes
Μέλαμπες

Ágios Dim

Agroúles

Káto
Saktoúria

Áno
Saktoúria

Vouvála
947 m

Ligres Beach

90 m

Triópetra
Beach

449 m

Ágios
Geórgios

137

Ágios Pávlos

Prasoní

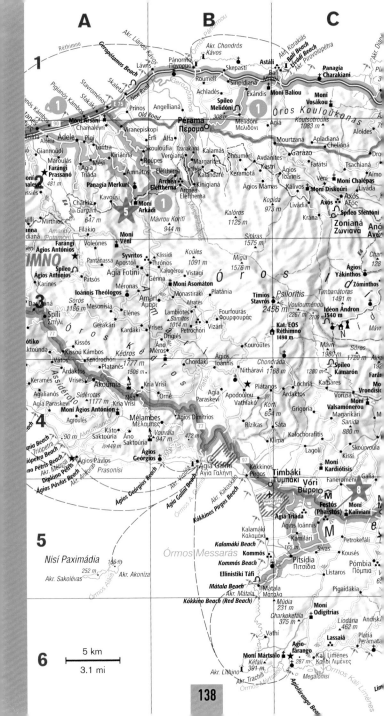

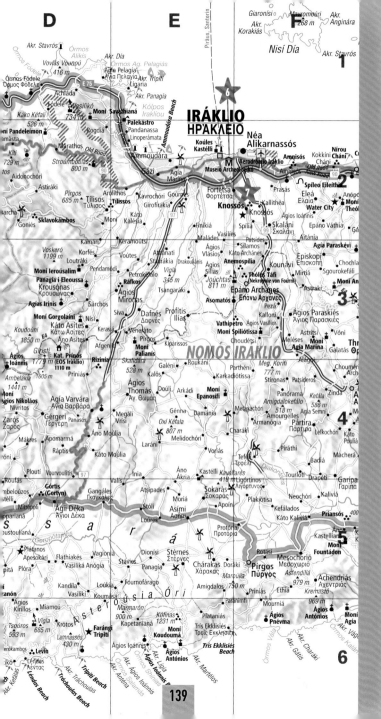

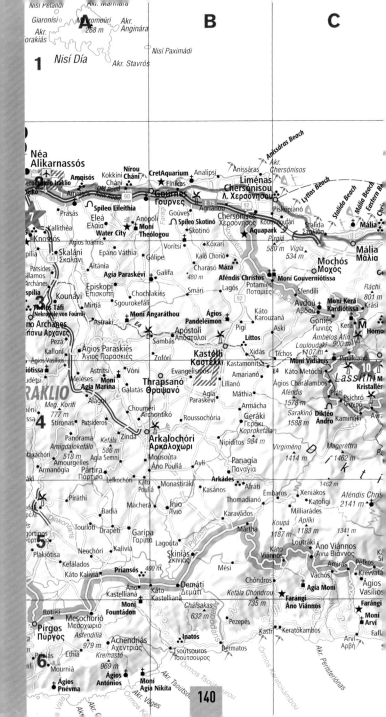

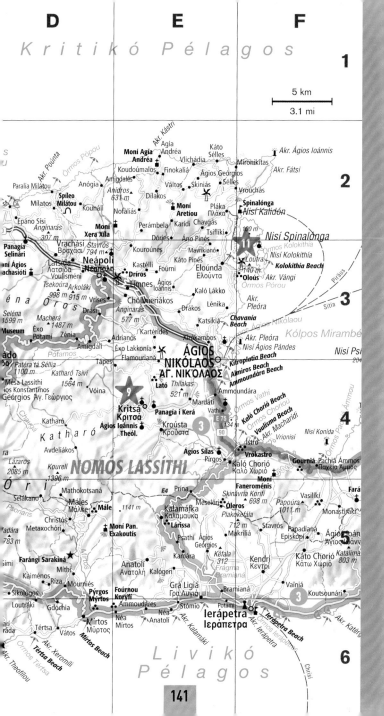

1

Kritikó Pélagos

5 km
3.1 mi

2

Akr. Poúnta
Ormós Pópou
Paralia Milátou
Milatos
**Spíleo
Milátou**
Kounáli
Akr. Kástri
Anógia
Amigdalés
*Anídros
631 m*
Dílakos
Váltos
Skiniás
Koudoúmalos
Finokaliá
**Moní Agía
Andréa**
Agía
Andréa
Vlichádia
Káto
Sélles
Ágios Geórgios
Sélles
Míronikítas
Akr. Ágios Ioánnis
Akr. Fátsi
Vrouchás

Epáno Sísi
Anginarás
307 m
Nofaliás
Perámbela
**Moní
Aretíou**
Pláka
Pláka
Karídi
Chavgás
Tsiflíki
Spinalónga
Nisí Kalídon

**Panagía
Selinári**
ní Ágios
achasióti
Latsída
Λατσίδα
Voulisméni
**Vrachási
Βραχάσι**
*Stavrós
794 m*
**Moní
Xerá Xíla**
Kouroúnes
Kastélli
Foúrni
Áno Pinés
Káto Pinés
Mavrikianó
100 m
11
Loútra
140 m
Nisí Spinalónga
Ormós Kolokithía
Kolokithía Beach

2

*na
Óros*
*Seléna
1599 m*
*Macherá
1487 m*
**Neápoli
Νεάπολη**
Arkoláki
Tsekoúra
998 m   915 m
Vríses
Drási
Dríros
Límnes
Choumeriákos
*Anginarás
577 m*
Ágios
Ioánnis
Drákos
Lénika
Eloúnta
Ελούντα
Kaló Lákko
Katsikiá
**Chavanía
Beach**
*Akr.
Pleóra*
Oloús Akr. Vángi
Ormós Pórou
Piraus
Sitía

3

*Ó r i
Oros*
Museum
*Éxo
Potamí*
Zénia
Adrianós
Amigdáli
Éxo Lakkonía
Flamouriané
Karterídes
Xirókambos
**ÁGIOS
NIKÓLAOS
ΑΓ. ΝΙΚΌΛΑΟΣ**
Akr. Pleóra
Nisí Ágios Pándes
Akr. Nikólaou
Kólpos Mirambé
Nisí Psi
204

*Patéra tá Séllia
1100 m*
*Mésa Lassíthi
ios Konstantínos
Geórgios Αγ. Γεώργιος*
*Katharó Tsiví
1564 m*
Vóina
Lató
*Thílakas
521 m*
9
**Kritsá
Κριτσά**
**Ágios Ioánnis
Theól.**
Panagía i Kerá
Kroústa
Κρούστα
3
Mardáti
Vathí
Ammoundára
Kitroplatía Beach
Almiros Beach
Ammoundára Beach
Ormós Vathí
Kaló Chorió Beach
Ormós Choriou
Voulisma Beach
Akr. Macharídi
Nisí Konída
4

Katharó
Avdeliákos
NOMOS LASSÍTHI
Ágios Sílas
Pírgos
Vrókastro
Kaló Chorió
Καλό Χωριό
Gournia
Pachiá Ámmos
Παχειά Άμμος

ra
*Lázaros
2085 m*
Kourelí
1396 m
Mathokotsaná
Prína
**Moni
Fanerménis**
*Skinavria Korifí
698 m*
Vasilikí
Fará

Óri
Selákano
Psonaris
**Máles
Μάλες**
Mále
1141 m
Meselérí
Kalamáfka
Καλαμαύκα
Óleros
*Plakokéfala
712 m*
*Papoúra
1011 m*
Papadianá
Monastiráki
5

*adára
783 m*
Christós
Metaxochóri
**Moní Pan.
Exakoútis**
Lárissa
Psathí
Ágios
Geórgios
Makrillá
Stavrós
Episkopí
**Ágios ván
Άγιος**
*Katalíma
803 m*

imi
Farángi Sarakiná
Mithrí
Kámenos
Ríza
Mourniés
Anatolí
Ανατολή
Kalógeri
Kamára
*Kéfala
312*
Kendrí
Κεντρί
**Káto Chorió
Κάτω Χωριό**

ári
ráda
Loutráki
Gdóchia
**Pýrgos
Mýrtos**
Foúrnou
Korýfi
Ammoudáres
Néa
Grá Ligiá
Γρα Λυγιά
*Fragma
Bramianá*
Bramianá
Vainiá
3
Koutsounári

Tértsa
Vátos
**Mírtos
Μύρτος**
Néa
Mírtos
Stómio
Anatolí
Akr. Kalamáki
Potamí
**Ierápetra
Ιεράπετρα**
Ierápetra Beach
ios Ierapetras
Akr. Ierápetra
Akr. Kater

6

Mírtos Beach
Akr. Xeromíli
Tértsa Beach
Ormós Tértsa
Akr. Theofílou

*Liviko
Pélagos*

Chrisi

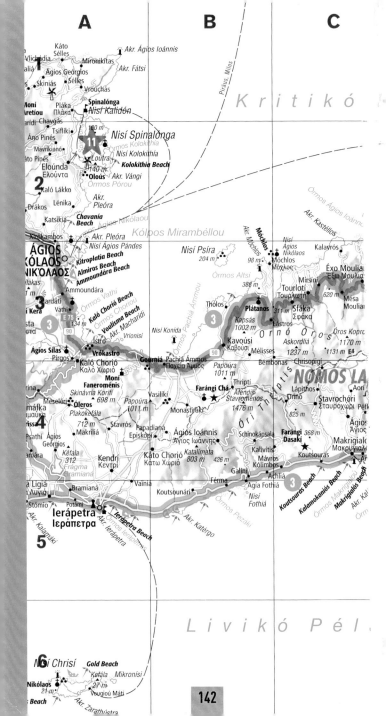

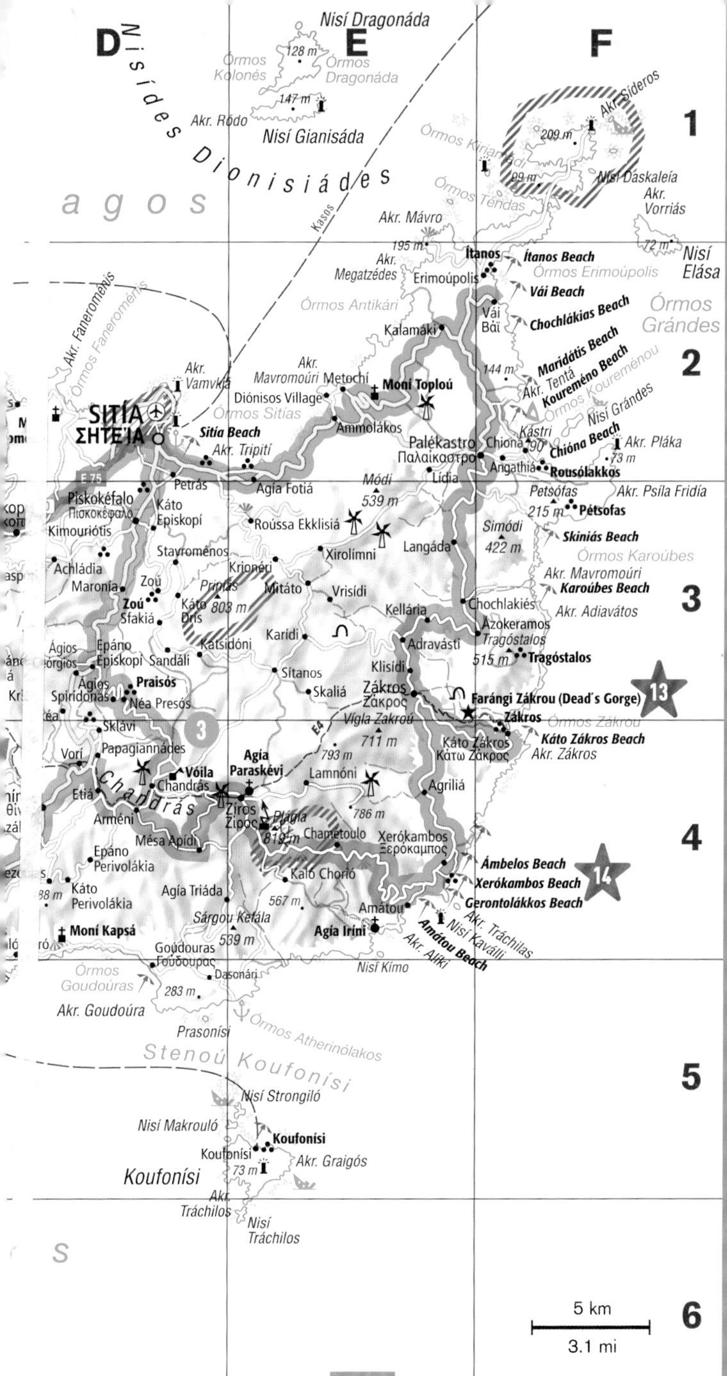

D
E
F
1
2
3
4
5
6
Nisí Dragonáda
Nisídes Dionisiádes
Órmos Kolonés
Órmos Dragonáda
128 m
147 m
Akr. Ródo
Nisí Gianisáda
Kasos
Akr. Síderos
209 m
Órmos Kiriamádi
99 m
Nisí Daskaleía
Akr. Vorriás
Órmos Téndas
Akr. Mávro
195 m
72 m
Nisí Elása
Ítanos
Ítanos Beach
Órmos Erimoúpolis
Akr. Megatzédes
Erimoúpolis
Vái Beach
Órmos Antikári
Vái
Βάι
Chochlákias Beach
Órmos Grándes
Akr. Faneroménis
Órmos Faneroménis
Kalamáki
Maridátis Beach
144 m
Akr. Tentá
Kouremeno Beach
Órmos Koureménou
Nisí Grándes
Akr. Vamvkiá
Akr. Mavromoúri
Metochí
Moní Toplóu
Diónisos Village
SITÍA
ΣΗΤΕΊΑ
Órmos Sitías
Ammolákos
Sitía Beach
Akr. Tripití
Palékastro
Παλαίκαστρο
Chióna
Kástri
90
Chióna Beach
Akr. Pláka
73 m
Angathiá
Rousólakkos
Lídia
E 75
Petrás
Agía Fotiá
Módi
539 m
Petsófas
Akr. Psíla Fridía
Piskokéfalo
Πισκοκέφαλο
Káto Episkopí
215 m
Pétsofas
Kimouriótis
Roússa Ekklisiá
Simódi
422 m
Skiniás Beach
Langáda
Xirolímni
Stavroménos
Órmos Karoúbes
Achládia
Krionéri
Akr. Mavromoúri
Karoúbes Beach
Maronía
Zoú
Priniás
Mitáto
Vrisídi
Zoú
Sfakiá
Káto Dris
803 m
Chochlakiés
Akr. Adiavátos
Kellária
Azokeramos
Karídi
Tragóstalos
Ágios Geórgios
Epáno Episkopí
Sandáli
Katsidóni
Adravásti
515 m
Tragóstalos
Klisídi
Ágios Spirídonas
Praisós
Néa Presós
Sítanos
Skaliá
Zákros
Ζάκρος
Farángi Zákrou (Dead's Gorge)
13
Zákros
Órmos Zákrou
Sklávi
3
Vígla Zakroú
711 m
E4
Káto Zákros
Κάτω Ζάκρος
Káto Zákros Beach
Akr. Zákros
Vorí
Papagiannádes
793 m
Vóila
Agía Paraskévi
Lamnóni
Chandrás
Etiá
Chandrás
Agriliá
Ziros
Ζίρος
Plágia
786 m
Arméni
819 m
Chamétoulo
Xerókambos
Ξερόκαμπος
Mésa Apídi
Epáno Perivolákia
Ámbelos Beach
14
Kaló Chorió
Xerókambos Beach
Káto Perivolákia
Agía Triáda
567 m
Gerontolákkos Beach
Amátou
Akr. Tráchilas
Sárgou Kefála
Nisí Kaválli
Moní Kapsá
539 m
Agía Iríni
Amátou Beach
Akr. Alíki
Goúdouras
Γούδουρας
Dasonári
Nisí Kímo
Órmos Goudoúras
283 m
Akr. Goudoúra
Prasonísi
Órmos Atherinólakos
Stenoú Koufonísi
Nisí Strongiló
Nisí Makrouló
Koufonísi
Koufonísi
73 m
Akr. Graigós
Koufonísi
Akr. Tráchilos
Nisí Tráchilos
5 km
3.1 mi

KEY TO ROAD ATLAS

Motorway with number
Autobahn mit Nummer

Clearway
Schnellstraße

Highway with number
Fernstraße mit Nummer

Main road with number
Hauptstraße mit Nummer

Secondary road
Nebenstraßen

Road unpaved
Straße ungeteert

Road under construction; projected
Straße in Bau; in Planung

Carriage way
Fahrweg

District border
Distriktgrenze

Prohibited area
Sperrgebiet

National park, nature reserve
Nationalpark, Naturreservat

Coral reef
Korallenriff

Youth hostel
Jugendherberge

Marina
Jachthafen

Anchorage, harbour
Ankerplatz, Hafen

Skin diving
Schnorcheln

Diving
Tauchen

Windsurfing
Windsurfing

Water skiing
Wasserski

Castle; castle ruin
Burg; Burgruine

Palace
Schloss

Church; church ruin
Kirche; Kirchenruine

Monastery; monastery ruin
Kloster; Klosterruine

Monument
Denkmal

Tower
Turm

Lighthouse
Leuchtturm

Wind engines
Windräder

Aerial mast
Sendemast

Point of interest
Sehenswürdigkeit

Archeological site
Archäologische Stätte

Mountain hut
Berghütte

Mountain top; geodetic point
Berggipfel; Höhenpunkt

Pass
Pass

Cavern
Höhle

Panoramic view
Aussichtspunkt

Beach
Badestrand

International airport
Internationaler Flughafen

Aerodrome
Flugplatz

Trips & tours
Ausflüge & Touren

Perfect route
Perfekte Route

MARCO POLO Highlight

INDEX

This index lists all places and sights, plus the names of important people featured in this guide. Numbers in bold indicate a main entry.

WRITE TO US

e-mail: info@marcopologuides.co.uk

Did you have a **great** holiday?
Is there something on your mind?
Whatever it is, let us know!
Whether you want to praise, alert us
to errors or give us a personal tip –
MARCO POLO would be pleased to
hear from you.
W̶ ̶d̶ everything we can to provide the

Nevertheless, despite all of our authors'
thorough research, errors can creep in.
MARCO POLO does not accept any
liability for this. Please contact us by
e-mail or post.

MARCO POLO Travel Publishing Ltd
Pinewood, Chineham Business Park
Crockford Lane, Chineham
Basingstoke, Hampshire RG24 8AL

38, 41, 56, 60,
fotolia.com:
ein (108/109),
19), Johanna
7, 8, 26 right);
Alamy (Front
ight, 2 Centre
/71, 72/73, 74,
Mevald (16 M.)

com

Chief editors: Michaela Lienemann (concept, managing editor), M̶   )
Author: Klaus Bötig
Editors: Christina Sothmann, Marlis v. Hessert-Fraatz
Programme supervision: Ann-Katrin Kutzner, Nikolai Michaelis, Silwen Randebrock
Picture editor: Gabriele Forst
What's hot: wunder media, Munich
Cartography road atlas & pull-out map: DuMont Reisekartografie, Fürstenfeldbruck; © MAIRDUMONT, Ostfildern
Design: milchhof : atelier, Berlin; Front cover, pull-out map cover, page 1: factor product munich
Translated from German by Wendy Barrow; editor of the English edition: Margaret Howie, fullproof.co.za
Prepress: M. Feuerstein, Wigel
Phrase book in cooperation with Ernst Klett Sprachen GmbH, Stuttgart, Editorial by Pons Wörterbücher

DOS & DON'TS ✋

Even in Crete, there are a few things you should bear in mind

DON'T UNDERESTIMATE THE DANGER OF FIRES

The risk of a forest fire on Crete is high and smokers must be especially careful and should never discard their cigarettes butts.

DO PARK LEGALLY

Parking illegally is very expensive: 80 euros is what this indulgence will cost you. Other traffic violations are also heavily fined.

DON'T BE SHOCKED BY THE PRICE OF FISH

Fresh fish is very expensive and is often sold by weight. Always ask for the kilo price first and when the fish is being weighed, make sure you are present to avoid any unpleasant surprises.

DO COVER UP IN THE CHURCHES

Cretans are used to seeing some skin in the beach resorts but in the villages, you should dress more conservatively. In the churches and monasteries it is expected that knees and shoulders be covered.

DON'T TAKE ARTEFACTS

On the beach and in the mountains no one will mind if you collect a pebble or two but taking a stone that has been crafted into something or ceramic shards from an archaeological site is an offence.

DO PAY THE COVER CHARGE

Most restaurant bills have some incomprehensible entries: 0.25–2 euros per person cover charge. Theoretically this cost is for cutlery, bread and serviettes. It is a general charge and even if you do not use any cutlery or eat any bread, you have to pay it.

DON'T PHOTOGRAPH WITHOUT PERMISSION

Many Cretans love to have their photograph taken, but dislike tourist that act as though they are on safari. Before you just start snapping away, smile at the person you want to photograph and wait for their permission.

DON'T EXPECT FRESH CALAMARI

Many tourists love eating calamari. It is very tasty but it seldom comes from Greek waters (it's usually from India). In the honest restaurants and tavernas, frozen foods are indicated – in the Greek section of the menu – with the letters 'kat'.

DO STAY ON THE TARMAC

If you are travelling with a hired vehicle and leave the main road, you will be driving without insurance and will have to pay for any damages yourself. That sometimes also even goes for 4 × 4 vehicles! Windshield damage is not insured even if the damage occurred on a tarmac road.